G·O·U·R·M·E·T
PRESERVES
CHEZ
MADELAINE

MADELAINE BULLWINKEL

Contemporary Books, Inc.
Chicago

Library of Congress Cataloging in Publication Data

Bullwinkel, Madelaine.
  Gourmet preserves chez Madelaine.

  Includes index.
  1. Jam.   2. Jelly.   I. Title.
TX612.J3B85   1984   641.8'52   84-12641
ISBN 0-8092-5482-4

Published by Contemporary Books, Inc.
180 North Michigan Avenue, Chicago, Illinois 60601
Manufactured in the United States of America
Library of Congress Catalog Card Number: 84-12641
International Standard Book Number: 0-8092-5482-4

Published simultaneously in Canada by Beaverbooks, Ltd.
195 Allstate Parkway, Valleywood Business Park
Markham, Ontario L3R 4T8 Canada

To my parents,
William and Mary de Huszar

CONTENTS

ACKNOWLEDGMENTS

First to receive my thanks are Phylis Magida and Rick Vittenson, whose interest in my preserving style produced the idea for this book. From the first jam to the last trifle, Charlotte Finley was there to test and taste many experiments. Kathleen German helped develop the no-sugar jams, and Jean Beck assisted in troubleshooting the last few stubborn recipes. My friends Paula Solinger, Pat Opler, and Marlene Rogers also tested recipes, shared their opinions, and gave me support.

I have modern Muses to thank for helping me give clear expression to my food ideas in both pen and print. Henrietta Tweedie gave sound advice that guided my pen through the illustrations. Nao Hauser nurtured the author as she expertly edited the text. And my husband George, working behind the scenes, proved to be the best ingredient for success any wife could hope for.

1

INTRODUCTION

The anticipation of pleasure always draws me to gourmet shop displays of jams, jellies, marmalades, and preserves. But in the end I always leave empty-handed. And it's not just because these products are always so expensive. More important, I know too well that they will never taste as good as my own homemade preserves.

Jams and jellies are also easy and satisfying work. When you start with small quantities of fruit and ordinary home equipment the preserving process moves along much more quickly than it can in a commercial operation. So you can avoid the long cooking time that robs fruit of its unique flavor. You can use less sugar or even none at all. And best of all, you can freely explore a spectrum of new flavor combinations.

This book is designed to relieve any uncertainty or concern you may have about fruit preserving. I have specified exact amounts of fruit, the time to allow for each cooking process, and the volume of finished preserve you can expect. You will also learn to jell preserves without having to use processed pectin such as Certo and Sure-Jell. And that will be a welcome change for those of you who know the great amount of sugar these products require.

This desire to preserve fresh fruits and incorporate them into our food lives has a long history marked by sudden dramatic innovations. From the time when our ancestors first had a surplus of food, methods have been developed to preserve abundant harvest for later consumption. Our prescien-

1

tific forebearers knew that warm air and moisture provide a playground for the destructive activity of molds, yeasts, and bacteria. So they froze fruits, vegetables, meats, and fish in cold areas and air-dried them in hot, arid climates. Meat was sometimes soaked in a heavy brine to preserve it or hung over a slow fire to dry.

The Romans sealed fresh figs, pears, and plums in honey, not realizing that raw produce can still decay from within in the absence of air. Evidence of the first cooked fruit preserved in sugar comes from the early years of the Italian Renaissance. The fruits are described in Boccaccio's fourteenth-century writing as romantic, luxurious fare for the aristocracy. At that time sugar was imported from the Near East through Venice; it remained rare and quite expensive through the eighteenth century.

By the middle of the sixteenth century, translations of Italian cookbooks with recipes for preserves began to appear in France. The first instance of a *marmalet* in an English cookbook dates from the early 1500s. Its source was a Portuguese recipe for preserved *marmelo* quince.

Sweet preserves graced the royal tables of Europe with increasing regularity as their popularity spread northward. When the New World was cultivated, sugar became a staple crop, and preserves became part of the European legacy. Many islands in the Caribbean grew generous sugar crops using slave labor. There were also good-sized sugar plantations in Louisiana, Alabama, Florida, Georgia, and Mississippi before the Civil War. But the sugar content of American crops was lower than that grown in the West Indies, so the United States imported cheap molasses from the islands to meet its sugar needs. Only in the middle nineteenth century was an inexpensive method for processing cane sugar perfected. On the heels of this discovery came the burgeoning production of sugar from beets. Now many more households could afford to experience the pleasures of preserves.

In 1810, in France, Nicholas Appert invented a method for canning in glass jars. But it took the ingenuity of three Americans to perfect the vacuum seal. John Mason first patented a glass jar with threaded top and airtight metal cap. The Ball brothers picked up Mason's designs when his patents expired and continued to make Mason's jars. In 1915 John Kerr bought the rights to a German heat-sealing gasket on a lacquered metal lid that would vent air when heated and then seal quickly when cooled. Today we buy Ball's version of the Mason jar with a Kerr screw cap lid.

The invention of the vacuum sealable jar had an effect similar to the drop in sugar prices. It made fruit preserving more accessible to homemakers. It also allowed for the safe and inexpensive manufacture of preserves on a large commercial scale. More and more people took advantage of the opportunity to purchase preserves, though homemade preserves continued to be a staple in rural communities and among those who carried on family cooking traditions.

Early in this century the natural jelling substance in fruit, called *pectin,* was isolated and processed for commercial preservers. Pectin was also introduced to housewives as a foolproof way to make jellies, marmalades, and preserves. There were now two schools of preserving: the old-fashioned way that depended on natural pectin and the new way that utilized processed pectin.

In 1974 the sale of glass jars by the Ball Corporation rose 2,500 percent. The people who had returned to home gardening in the early 1970s were learning to preserve the economy and honesty of their new cuisine for the winter. The rise in home preserving was, in part, symptomatic of a period of national self-scrutiny in America. We questioned the environmental quality in our cities, the use of pesticides in farming, and the presence of additives and chemical preservatives in processed foods.

Commercial processors responded to the popular demand for purer foods. But commercial preserves still offer less flavor and fewer nutritional benefits than homemade. They are turned out in mass quantities. Juices are extracted under pressure, destroying their natural jelling ability. To compensate for this loss, many brands of preserves are infused with processed pectin, which jells with a vengeance and requires excessive amounts of sugar. The result is a preserved product that tastes first and foremost of sugar, with the fruit flavor running a poor second. Often the pectin itself leaves a harsh metallic aftertaste.

Some "natural" brands advertise that they contain no artificial pectin and less sugar. But federal guidelines recommend the presence of at least 55 percent sugar in commercially-made preserves and jellies. And, new products with modified jells usually have a loose or sloppy consistency. The buyer should beware! Thin preserves not only look unappetizing; they can also leave a sticky trail from lap to lips.

The home cook has several advantages over the commercial mass producer. He or she can work in small quantities—four to six cups of fruit and juice—in a modestly equipped kitchen. Cooking is quick and easy, and juices can be reduced to produce a desirable natural pectin level. Sugar can be added as needed without slowing the process. The resulting jam or jelly always has an intense, fresh flavor. And because it has been made in small quantities, each preserve can be eaten within a month or two, inspiring yet another batch of seasonal offerings.

Despite the basic simplicity of the preserving process just described, I looked in vain for a consistent, up-to-date guide to preserving with sugar when I first began to make jams and jellies. I loved to bake my own breads and wanted to complement them with fresh fruit preserves. I found that I had to sift among a maze of pickling and canning techniques to find recipes for jams and jellies in the many books on preserving. The recipes themselves were either the old-fashioned kind, calling for large quantities of fruit and offering no specific cooking times and yields, or they were the new variety that used processed pectin and lots of sugar.

As I read and experimented on my own, I learned that pectin, a high-fiber carbohydrate found in most fruits, could be isolated, weighed, and measured in my own kitchen. When I began making tests for pectin, I discovered that some fruits with a poor reputation for pectin content really had a sufficient amount if cooked in small quantities and reduced a bit. By pairing high- and low-pectin fruits, I was able to make unusual taste combinations, ones I had not seen in the books I consulted. I had great fun creating such irresistible novelties as Kiwifruit and Pineapple Jam, Ratatouille Marmalade, and Tomato and Prune Jam (see index); but it was no less exhilarating to taste the differences wrought simply by adding the scent of vanilla to pineapple preserves and the zing of fresh ginger to blackberry preserves.

As I cooked the fruit juices with sugar to make a jell, I found that the vague techniques described in the old-fashioned recipes needed to be revised and clearly defined. For example, the spoon test, plate test, and thermometer test, considered the three standard ways to check a jell, were not equally reliable. I found, to my horror, that the most accurate measuring device, the thermometer, was, more often than not, inaccurate!

I have developed ways of making the jelling process measurable and exact. For beginners this means new cooking pleasure without guesswork as well as joyous eating for family and friends. For the experienced preserver I offer a thorough understanding of what you've been doing right (or sometimes wrong) all these years and some unusual taste treats.

I have kept sugar to a minimum in all these recipes. There is even a section on no-sugar jams (Chapter 4), which combine unsweetened fruit juice concentrates and canned fruit with fresh and dried fruits. The sweetness in these jams comes from their natural fruit sugar, called *fructose*. In the section on preserves I have devised a new technique that yields sparkling fruit pieces suspended in jelly and requires far less sugar than the old method in which fruits were cooked and steeped in a heavy sugar syrup. Not new, but applied in new ways is my formula for Pectin Stock. This natural pectin-booster is made from the concentrated juice of tart apples. I like to use it as a base for rich wine jellies, as variations to the theme of orange marmalade, and as a freshener for the taste of strawberry preserves.

The last two chapters of this book are devoted to breads, muffins, and desserts. They contain a wealth of answers to the question I sometimes hear, "What can I do with this jam?" They will help you extend the use of your preserves beyond breakfast and tea, into brunch, lunch, and dinner. In them you will find wonderful recipes for fruit sauces, sorbets, and ice cream as well as a pastry cart full of other ideas for showing off your homemade preserves.

HOW TO USE THIS BOOK

Chapter 2 combines a general introduction to my preserving method with a description of the preserving process, important ingredients, and necessary equipment. After you familiarize yourself with the chemistry of the jell and the practical matters of executing a recipe, you will be ready to move on to the recipes that follow.

Each recipe chapter (Chapters 3-7) focuses on a single preserving technique, with an introduction that details procedure and tips on improvising. The chapters and recipes appear in order of difficulty. First are fruit jams made from chopped, mashed, or puréed fruit pieces cooked with sugar. The process of transforming cooked, strained fruit juices into crystal-clear jelly is next. The chapter on marmalades lists the various ways to develop flavor, all of which produce a shimmering jelly filled with bits of citrus peel, fruit, or even an occasional vegetable. A collection of rich fruit preserve recipes with their chunks of fruit in tender jelly ends this portion of the book.

Every recipe repeats pertinent information on equipment sizes and materials. The procedure for filling jars and sealing them also appears. Refer to Chapter 2 with additional questions you may have.

The last two chapters in this book are intended to be used after you make any one of the preserves in this book. They include quick bread recipes and desserts that will give you many opportunities to serve your jams and jellies with panache. The introductory notes to these recipes offer technical help, tips on improvising, and serving ideas.

The Appendix lists the seasonal availability of the fruits and vegetables featured in the recipes as well as a description of their appearance at peak ripeness.

With the thoroughly tested recipes in this book you can look forward to experiencing the magnified scents and flavors of fresh fruits in more than 100 luscious jams, jellies, marmalades, and preserves. For me, eating them recalls berry-stained fingers and the warm breath of sunny orchards at harvest. What a pleasure it is to satisfy one's appetite, entertain friends, and ease the passage of time with this sweet celebration of nature's bounty!

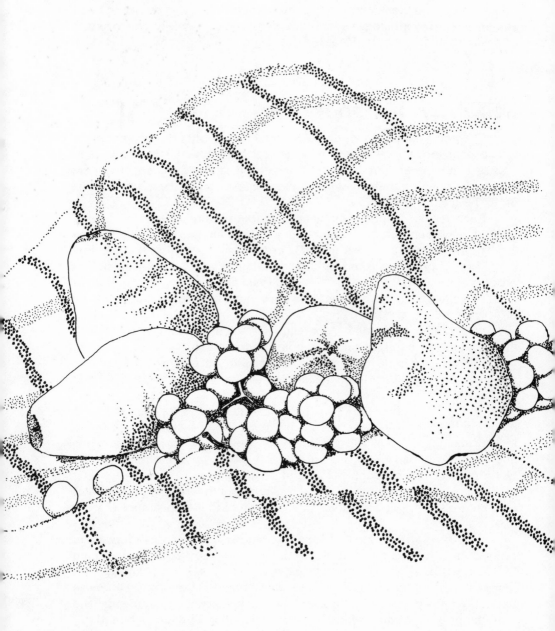

2

TECHNIQUE AND EQUIPMENT FOR PRESERVING

A good preserve requires a unique balance of ingredients. Pectin, acid, and sugar levels all have to be in the proper proportion. And these elements are not standardized. They vary in fruits and berries from season to season, from year to year, from variety to variety, and from growing area to growing area.

The unpredictability of pectin and acid levels can cause problems in mass production, but the issue is quite manageable when a cook is working in small amounts. The techniques used in this book take into account the natural variability of fruits and recognize as well the unique character of each category of preserving, offering consistency without compromising flavor.

All the recipes in this book have been carefully tested to produce satisfying preserves. In each recipe a preliminary cooking time, the procedure for adding

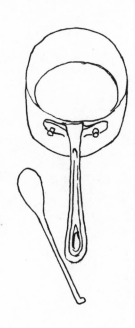

7

sugar, and a final cooking period are repeated along with instructions for cleaning empty jars and processing full ones. You will be able to get good results simply by following directions.

Throughout this book I also encourage you to experiment with seasonings and with fruit combinations. To cook creatively, you need to know more about how and why the various preserving techniques work. This chapter on technique and equipment is designed to help you familiarize yourself with the chemistry and execution of pectin jells. To streamline the learning process, equipment descriptions appear right next to the technical explanations.

SELECTING FRUIT FOR PRESERVING

If you plan to concoct your own preserve recipes, you must understand the importance of pectin level in order to choose successful fruit combinations. Even if you use only the recipes in this book, you should understand how jelly becomes jelly so that you can select the best-quality fruits at your market, or make a last-minute fruit substitution.

The highest priority in fruit preserving is the selection of fresh, unblemished fruits and berries that are just at their peak of ripeness. We can't expect cooking techniques to improve flavor; we hope simply to preserve it. Use the same fruit variety as that in the recipe unless an alternative is given. If no option is mentioned, choose the freshest and firmest one available. Check "A Seasonal Guide to Fresh Fruits and

Vegetables for Preserving" (Appendix) for specifics on when to preserve each fruit and how to judge its ripeness. This is especially true for recipes that jell; that is, jellies, marmalades, and preserves. A soft apple like the MacIntosh will not cook to the same consistency or have the same pectin level as a firmer, tarter Granny Smith or Jonathan apple.

You may be surprised to learn later in this chapter how underripe fruit aids the jelling of many low-pectin fruits in preserve recipes. At this point we will simply mention that up to 25 percent half-ripe fruits can be used to boost the pectin and acid levels in such fruits as pears, peaches, apricots, rhubarb, figs, pineapple, and strawberries. On the other hand, overripe fruit that quickly loses its shape and flavor when cooked is never appropriate for preserving.

Fresh vs. Frozen

If fresh produce is unavailable, frozen fruits may be substituted. These fruit pieces must be frozen individually without a sugar syrup and fully thawed before you begin cooking. Defrosted berries will exude more juice because freezing and thawing have damaged their cell structure. Count on an additional 5-10 minutes to reduce juices.

Also keep in mind that frozen fruit will come without the core, pit, or stone that is present in a fresh one. You will have to estimate the weight of the missing parts and either add less frozen fruit or add more of the other ingredients to the recipe. I would advise you with a fruit such as apricots, for example, to use 20 percent fewer frozen

An optional but highly desirable piece of equipment is a beam balance scale that will measure up to 20 pounds. With an exact scale, you can measure ingredients and duplicate recipes with greater ease.

apricot slices than you would fresh apricots with their pits intact (or increase the sugar, water, and seasoning in the recipe by 20 percent). There is, of course, no weight difference between fresh and frozen dry-packed berries.

There is frequently a loss of taste in commercially frozen fruit. You will want to cool and taste spoonfuls of these juices throughout the cooking process and make appropriate changes in flavorings. Taste may be accentuated by reducing the preserve further or by decreasing the acid and seasonings to balance a more fragile flavor.

Fruit juices that have been cooked and strained from fresh fruit can easily be frozen for future preserving. Let them defrost slowly in a refrigerator overnight before cooking.

The Chemistry of the Pectin Jell

After fruit is cooked for 10 minutes its natural pectin is activated. This pectin factor determines the amount of sugar and acid necessary to form a jell in jellies, marmalades, and preserves.

Even today most descriptions of pectin jell chemistry are clouded in mystery. What actually happens to pectin during a jell, and how can we apply the chemistry of this event to a real recipe? With this book the link between chemistry theory and practice should become clear to you.

In the past cooks had to rely on traditional recipes without ever knowing quite why they worked. Those who wanted the security of foolproof results learned to rely on commercial pectins such as Certo and Sure-Jell. But they are only crutches, and you can throw them away once you understand the basic roles of pectin, sugar, and acid in the preserving process. It's the only way to get fresher, more flavorful results.

Pectin is a fibrous carbohydrate bulging with entrapped water molecules. All fruits contain it in varying amounts, with higher concentrations in unripe stages tending to decline as the fruit ripens. High levels of pectin are found in fruits such as apples, currants, cranberries, blackberries, gooseberries, and quinces. The citrus fruits—orange, grapefruit, lemon, and lime—carry pectin in their bitter peels and pips (seeds). They are considered to have fair-to-good pectin levels as do grapes, plums, and raspberries. Fruits low in pectin include apricots, cherries, figs, pears, peaches, pineapple, rhubarb, and strawberries.

All fruits must be cooked for 10 minutes before the pectin is shaken loose enough to be measured easily. If a little acid is present in this heated solution, the pectin will also change its molecular structure and physical properties, becoming less possessive of its water and more attracted to other pectin molecules. Add sugar to this solution, and a chemical reaction takes place.

Sugar breaks down in the presence of heat and an acid. It inverts to form the simple sugars, glucose and fructose. These sugars hungrily strip water molecules off the pectin chains. The unfettered pectins can then come together freely. This dense web of pectin that holds and supports the aqueous sugar is a jell.

Fruits with High Pectin Level

Apple
Blackberry
Crabapple
Cranberry
Red Currant
Grape
Quince
Red and Black
    Raspberry
Serviceberry

Testing for Jell

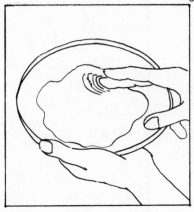

Cold Plate Test:
Jelly will wrinkle
on a cold plate if
it has jelled.

Spoon Test:
Preserves will fall
in a single sheet
at 216° F.

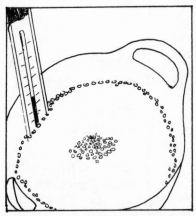

Thermometer Test:
Measure the
temperature of water
on your thermometer
at boiling (212° F.
at sea level).

Thermometer Test:
Test for the jelling
point adding 8° to
the temperature
reading on your ther-
mometer at boiling
(220°F. at sea level).

MEASURING THE PECTIN LEVEL IN FRUIT

I have measured the exact pectin levels in all the jelly, marmalade, and preserve recipes in this book, often more than once, to assure that the proportions of fruit, sugar, and acid will give you a jelled product. If you want to create a new recipe, you will want to make this pectin test yourself as you cook. Although pectin is invisible to the naked eye in fruit juices, it is possible to separate pectin from cooked juice and observe its concentration.

To do this pectin test, stir 1 tablespoon of the unsweetened, cooked fruit juice in question into a small, shallow bowl away from any heat source. Stir in 1½ tablespoons of grain alcohol (available at liquor stores) and let this mixture stand for one minute. As you pour it out on a plate, clear, congealed pectin will collect in lumps. The bigger the lumps, the higher the pectin content. (Illustrated on page 12.)

The degree of pectin lumping determines the proportion of sugar that will be added to the juice in each recipe to form a jell. For example, the strained juices of greening apples that I use to make apple jelly always form large pectin clumps.

Frequently pectin will form in distinct, smaller, but connected, lumps that can be picked up on a fork, indicating the jell potential is good but not sufficient. If the pectin masses are unrelated small lumps or ripples, as happens in recipes with pineapples, pears, and cherries, strong measures must be taken to raise the pectin

Fruits with Good Pectin Level

Boysenberry
Grapefruit
Lemon
Lime
Orange
Plum

Fruits with Low Pectin Level

Apricot
Blueberry
Cherry
Fig
Kiwifruit
Nectarine
Peach
Pear
Pineapple
Rhubarb
Strawberry

PRESERVING JARS AND LIDS

I distinguish between a ½-pint jelly jar with a snap-on lid and a quilted ½-pint (or quilted 12-ounce) jar with a vacuum-seal lid and screw-cap cover in all recipes. The jelly jars are recom-mended in the jelly and mar-malade recipes. A layer of paraffin on their surface will protect them from molds and yeast.

You can also use decorative jars or glasses for jelly and marmalade as long as the mouths of the jars do not narrow above the layer of wax, making it devilishly hard to remove.

level. We will discuss these remedies later in the chapter.

To understand fully their different sugar requirements, you may want to compare the look of natural pectin with the look of commercially processed pectin. Cook up a batch of Sure-Jell, let it cool a bit, and combine it with the alcohol as described. You will see the pectin rise out of the bowl as if it were a flexing muscle. It is just that. Imagine needing 1½ cups or more sugar per cup of juice to satisfy that tight wad of pectin!

Remember to throw out the alcohol test solutions without tasting it after these experiments. Grain alcohol has a 90 percent alcohol content. It is also quite flammable and should be stored in a cool spot.

RAISING PECTIN LEVELS IN FRUIT

There are several ways to boost the pectin content of fruit. I have already alluded to the art of combining a low with a high-pectin fruit in roughly equal amounts. The Blueberry Raspberry Preserves and the Pear and Grape Preserves (see index) are tasty examples.

Another approach is to use from 20–30 percent underripe fruit. This is particularly effective in the Italian Plum Preserves and Spicy Blueberry Preserves (see index), but it is not always sufficient by itself.

The most common technique I use to concentrate pectin strength for jelling is reducing the fruit juices by boiling off the excess liquid. Since we are working with only three to four pounds of fruit, this can be done quickly. A fruit or berry combination with good pectin strength to begin with, say one with red raspberries, will call for a reduction of less than a cup. A recipe with strawberries or pineapple will ask you to reduce strained juices by half at most.

How can you make preserves with low-pectin strawberries or blueberries or a jelly with wine that has no pectin at all? For these situations I have designed a Pectin Stock recipe (see index) capable of supplying all the pectin necessary for a jell.

The recipe for stock appears in the chapter with the jelly recipes because it is produced by straining apple juices from cooked fruit. Our master recipe uses Granny Smith apples, which are now available almost all year. However, the highest pectin levels are found in the sour greening apples. Since these are seasonal, a serious preserver will want to process a quantity when they are available and either vacuum-seal or freeze the stock. (Instructions are given for processing both kinds of apples; see Chapter 4.)

Pectin Stock may be refrigerated for two to three weeks, frozen up to six months, or vacuum-sealed indefinitely by processing it in a boiling water bath.

A good Pectin Stock can be made from the peels and pips of citrus fruits, but I prefer to use apple juices because their flavor and scent are less obtrusive.

This apple stock will have a high enough pectin strength to be the sole supply in our master Wine Jelly recipe (see index). I have added lesser amounts in marmalade and preserve recipes based on my appraisal of a pectin test of the juices.

POTS FOR STERILIZING JARS

You will need a large pot for sterilizing empty jars and vacuum-sealing full ones. The material, capacity, and dimensions of this container must meet two criteria. First, it should be broad enough to be fitted with a 10-inch round cake cooling rack. This rack will hold five pint or quart canning jars off the bottom of the pot without their touching one another. Second, the pot has to be deep enough to cover the tallest jars you use with an inch of water.

I use an aluminum spaghetti pot with a strainer

lining for boiling ½-pint jars. My 16-quart stock pot fitted with a cake rack handles larger and taller pint and quart preserving jars. Occasionally the racks may rust and color the water. Two tablespoons of distilled vinegar added to the water will dissolve the rust. Or you may wish to invest in a large preserving kettle with a removable tray.

MEASURING UTENSILS

Use heatproof glass measures to size up liquid ingredients and metal spoons and cups for dry ones. You will need three glass

The Role of Acid in the Jell

You should be aware that the acid in fruit is an important catalyst in the jelling process. Without an acid to reshape pectin and sugar molecules, jelling activity will be stymied. Many fruits have enough natural acid to transform the pectin. The easiest way to ensure natural sourness is simply to use some underripe fruit in these recipes. You will find that sweet and sour fruit combinations, as found in the Rhubarb Fig Jam (see index) are quite tasty, aside from being good chemistry. On some occasions I add lemon juice to assure good acidity, especially to naturally sweet low-pectin fruits such as the blueberries in the Spicy Blueberry Preserves (see index).

If you are experimenting with a new fruit or berry variety, taste the fruit before cooking it to ensure that it is slightly tart. If you are unsure, add 1 teaspoon of fresh lemon juice per pound of fruit when you begin cooking.

I introduce wine vinegar in the Prune Tomato Jam (see index) to make a more dramatic taste accent. You could experiment with any of the vinegars or citric acid to serve this role in preserving.

PREPARATION FOR PRESERVING

Set-Up Preserving Equipment

Before cooking the fruit, you will want to begin sterilizing the preserving jars and lids in boiling water so they will be hot and ready to be filled when the jam is finished cooking. Check jars to be sure that they are free of cracks or chips. While you wash and rinse the jars, bring enough water to cover the jars to a simmer in a large pot fitted with a rack. Submerge them in the pot for at least 15 minutes.

If you are making jams or preserves, check the manufacturer's instructions for sterilizing the lids. If there are none, dip lids in boiling water for 30 seconds and drain on a clean towel after removing the jars. Screw-caps for sealing the lids should be clean and free of rust. Give the plastic caps of jelly glasses a thorough washing.

Weighing and Measuring Ingredients

To assure the proper taste and consistency of a finished preserve, begin each recipe by carefully measuring and weighing the ingredients so that the basic proportions are followed. I have included the measured weight of fruit as well as specified the number of pieces or volume, because weight is a more accurate guide. Cup measurements are given for soft fruits or cooked fruit when there is little chance that the air spaces between pieces will greatly inflate the volume.

Sugar and liquids, on the other hand, are given as volume amounts because they are more easily and accurately measured in this form in American kitchens. Measure sugar in metal or plastic measures that are calibrated by weight. (One pound of sugar is 2¼ cups by volume.) Measure wet ingredients in clear, heatproof measures with spouts that are calibrated by volume.

measures: one-cup, two-cup, and one-quart. Use a set of nesting metal cups, including ¼, ½, and one cup. Also have on hand a variety of measuring spoons, from ¼ teaspoon to a tablespoon.

KNIVES

I highly recommend the purchase of both a high-carbon stainless steel chef's knife and a paring knife to prepare fruits quickly, easily, and safely for these recipes. Shop at a dependable cookware or cutlery store where the staff can explain to you the important features of a well-made knife. You want a knife with full tang (the metal should extend from the blade through the entire length of the handle). The knife should feel comfortable in your hand and be of sturdy hardwood or nonslip rubber material. Ask to be shown how and when to use a whetstone, sharpening steel, and a ceramic sharpener to maintain the cutting edge. Good knives are pricey additions to your kitchen stock but, if maintained, will give you a lifetime of good service.

Recipe yields are expressed in measured cups rather than the number of jelly jars, again for accuracy. Canning jars are never filled to their full half-pint or pint capacity.

Preparing Fruit for Cooking

Some chores, such as rinsing, removing stems, peeling, and coring, leave you no alternative but to work by hand with the fruit. Pare firm fruits such as pears and apples with a vegetable peeler. Dip thin-skinned fruits such as tomatoes, peaches, and apricots in boiling water for 30 seconds to loosen their skins. Then briefly cool them under running water to prevent the fruit flesh from being cooked. Now simply slip off the skins. To prevent apples from darkening after peeling, keep them in a bath of acidulated juice or water before cooking.

I recommend that you do much of the trimming, cutting, and slicing for small quantity fruit preserving by hand (as opposed to using a food processor). You can control the pressure on a good, sharp knife according to the texture of the fruit when cutting out a core, chopping, or slicing. The distinct fruit slices and diced pieces make an impression in the mouth that is essential to the sensuous appeal of the preserve.

The food processor *is* helpful when you want to chop finely a firm fleshed fruit, such as pineapple or apple or make a purée. Also, a thin slicing disc could be used to cut moderately firm peaches and pears, and the machine will come in handy to chop roughly whole citrus fruits.

The more specialized tools—a zester, stripper, or vegetable peeler (see illustration)—are called for in marmalade recipes to trim the outer peel from citrus fruits. Each kind of peel will contribute texture as well as aroma to the preserve.

Flavorings and Other Ingredients

HERBS AND SPICES IN PRESERVING

The imaginative use of fresh herbs, fine spices, and fragrant liqueurs in fruit preserves can greatly expand their expressive potential. For example, a sprig of fresh thyme in Grape Jelly (see index), a hint of Pernod with pear slices, and the scent of cardamom in Italian Plum Jam (see index) give an exciting new impression of each fruit and each preserve.

All the seasonings in these recipes, except for the tongue-tingling slices of fresh ginger, are ingredients we smell rather than taste. They are carried as volatile oils and can be driven off with excessive cooking. Fresh herbs are the most fragile. The recipes specify that they should be added near the end of the cooking process in the jelly and jam recipes. Crush and steep them for five minutes in the pot with a completed preserve; then remove them before pouring the preserve into jars.

The liqueurs are also added late in the cooking process or as the hot preserve is cooling. The goal is to warm the seasoned liquid enough to drive off the alcohol and yet retain its scent. You will need to taste a tablespoon of cooled preserve to which liqueurs have been added to see if the fragrance of the seasoning is in balance with the other ingredients. Adding a tablespoon

TOOLS FOR MARMALADE

One of the three handy little tools that remove the outer peel from citrus fruits will be required in most of the marmalade recipes. The stripper tool removes deep, narrow troughs of peel, while the vegetable peeler will simply skim the surface, removing just the colored surface layer. A zester tool has a row of tiny holes that scrape off the layers of colored peel into fragile slivers.

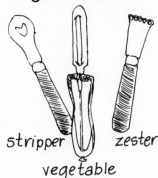

stripper   zester

vegetable
peeler

POTS FOR PRESERVING

Of prime importance to the preserver is a four- to five-quart saucepan or casserole in which to cook the fruit. It must be heavy and ovenproof. The pot should be deeper than it is wide and have a lid. The diameter of your vessel is also important. It should be no wider than the cooking burner on your range for best heat conduction, particularly on an electric stove.

My favorite materials are ceramic-coated cast iron and coated aluminum. The heat retention powers of cast iron are very welcome in preserving, and

or two of a liqueur will not change the consistency of the preserve. If you feel you have added too much seasoning, simply reheat the mixture to drive off its aromatic properties.

Spices are added at the beginning of the recipe and boiled in the preserves for the duration of the cooking time. Notice that I specify whole spices (versus ground) because they have good reserves of seasoning potential. The scent of ground herbs and spices in these recipes is too ephemeral. For example, basil loses important aromatic properties of its heady scent when it is dried, rendering it useless. (To assure the potency of their characteristic scents, replace your whole spices at least once a year.)

When there is more than one spice or the pieces are small, they are tied in cheesecloth so they can be easily removed later. I refer to this bundle of seasonings by the French name, *bouquet garni,* an aromatic garnish.

Fresh ginger root is even more perishable than the dried spices. Select plump, firm pieces of this knobby root. Keep it tied in plastic wrap in a refrigerator bin between uses and replace it when mold appears. Or preserve ginger by submerging it in a jar filled with sherry, removing it as needed to cut thin slices.

THE ROLE OF SUGAR IN THE JELL

White granulated sugar, known as *sucrose,* is used most often to sweeten preserves. Other sugars in honey or corn syrup could replace up to one-half the volume of this sugar, but they require additional cooking time to evaporate their higher liquid content.

Sweets like honey, molasses, and brown sugar also introduce to preserves new tastes that alter our perception of the fruit's flavor. I use brown sugar only once, in the Tomato Prune Jam (see index), but there are other preserves to which it would be an enhancement, such as the rhubarb jams. Feel free to experiment with these other sweeteners by substituting them in gradually increasing amounts up to one-half the sucrose in these recipes. You're bound to find the balance that works well.

COOKING THE FRUIT

Initial Cooking

All fruits destined for preserves require an initial cooking using medium to high heat, to draw out juices, in a deep, heavy, nonreactive pot. All cooking times are expressed with a range of 3 to 5 minutes to allow for differing performances of gas and electric ranges.

A small amount of water or sugar is added to uncooked fruit in the jam recipes, to prevent scorching the pan during the first few minutes of cooking. Fruit for jelly recipes will be cooked vigorously so it exudes as much juice as possible. In addition to stirring, you will crush the fruit with a spoon along the sides of the pot. The pure juice from this first cooking is then strained into a bowl and cooled before the jelly technique continues.

In the berry preserve recipes, where we want to extract juice but preserve whole

the ceramic coating is nonporous and easy to maintain. Heavy aluminum pots are well known for their excellent heat conduction capacity, but they should be covered with a nonstick coating or stainless steel. A protective surface prevents a harmless but unattractive chemical reaction between the pot and its contents during which acid in the fruit strips a thin layer of oxide off untreated aluminum. (I have referred to these pots in the recipes simply as heavy and nonreactive.)

STRAINING JUICES

Use an old but unfrayed tea towel or fine mesh cheesecloth to line a sieve or chinois for straining juices. Wash the cheesecloth before using to remove sizing. Remember to dampen any cloth strainer before pouring jelly through it. Use wooden spoons and heat-resistant rubber spatulas, both with long handles, for stirring.

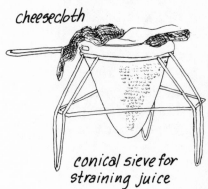

cheesecloth

conical sieve for straining juice

shapes, the fruit ingredients are baked rather than boiled. Specific timing and oven temperatures are given, but you will want to double check this procedure, too. The berries should be afloat in their juices when fully baked.

The next step is to stir all sugar into the boiling liquid one-half cup at a time. It must return to the boil before more sugar is added. This seemingly slow incorporation of small amounts of sugar is actually a time-saving measure, for it allows the preserves to return to the boil quickly. To speed cooking in recipes that add more than three cups of sugar, you will heat the sugar on a baking sheet for 10 minutes in a preheated 250° F. oven.

Cooking the Preserves to the Jell Point

An important factor in the jelling process is heat. A hot burner speeds cooking and preserves fruit flavor. The cook, however, has to be attentive and in control of the process. This need for precision is the best reason for working with small quantities.

In addition to stipulating the cooking time required to cook a jam (which does not jell) after all the sugar has been added (within a range of 3 to 5 minutes), I have often described the appearance and consistency of the cooked preserve so that the home cook can verify his or her work in two different ways. You can also check your completed jam by measuring it in a one-quart heatproof cup because every recipe includes a finished volume.

For those that jell there are several ways

to ensure that the preserve will cool to the desired consistency. Since you will use at least one test to verify the jell while the cooking is going on, you will have to be aware of how the specific tests work and how accurate their results are.

Testing for the Pectin Jell

Once the proper proportions of pectin, sugar, and acid are mixed, a jell will form. If left at room temperature, this process would occur over several days. Leaving the ingredients out in the hot summer sun, as some older recipes suggest, would produce a jell in a day or two. When we apply direct heat, however, the process speeds up dramatically. Forcing the molecules to fly about into one another in such an excited way makes the chemical reaction take place in minutes rather than hours. The next important question is: How does one know when to stop the process?

Three standard tests are used to check for the jell. They are the cold plate test, the spoon test, and the thermometer reading, all illustrated on page 24. You should know exactly how to make these tests as well as know their respective strengths and shortcomings.

COLD PLATE TEST

The cold plate test involves pouring just a few drops of hot jelly onto a cold plate, freezing it for a minute or two, and then observing how well it jells. The small puddle should chill to a semifirm consistency that does not run when tipped. A finger drawn

THERMOMETERS

A sturdy, easy-to-read thermometer is crucial to high-quality preserving. I prefer to use a candy thermometer consisting of a column of mercury set in a metal plate to measure the temperature of jellies and marmalade. You can clip it onto the side of the pan and watch it while the preserves cook.

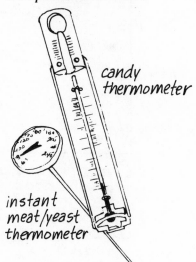

candy thermometer

instant meat/yeast thermometer

Testing for Pectin

Stir one tablespoon
of fruit juice into
one and one-half
tablespoons of
grain alcohol.

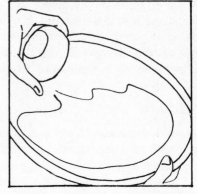

After one minute,
pour the mixture
onto a plate.

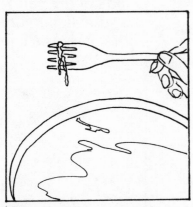

Connected strands
indicate good pectin
content. Reduce
juices by one-half
before adding
sugar.

Coherent masses of
pectin indicate
excellent jelling
potential. Use sugar
cup for cup with
juice.

through it should wrinkle the surface, indicating that a jell is forming.

The trouble with this method is that it takes valuable time at a critical point in the cooking process. A strong, active jell will begin to set in the pan while you are making the test. It will then develop a sea of tiny air bubbles in the jelly when it is poured into jars. This plate test has also falsely indicated a jell on more than one occasion. I consider it unreliable used by itself.

SPOON TEST

The spoon test also evaluates a preserve's viscosity. Here the cook dips a metal spoon into the hot jelly to fill it, then lets the liquid pour off to one side. If juices collect together and fall in a single sheet, the jelly is said to be done.

Having some jellies fail to jell after passing the spoon test, I double checked it with a thermometer. To my surprise I discovered that a jelly will pass the spoon test at 216° F., which is four degrees below the jell stage.

The spoon test turns out to be a good thickening indicator in jam recipes rather than in jelly and preserves. At 216° F. a richly textured mixture will cool to a thick, spreadable consistency.

THERMOMETER READING

You would think that we could trust a thermometer to measure the jell accurately and that a column of mercury will be an exact guide to the temperature change in a preserve, but it may not be correctly calibrated. One of my thermometers was off

Thick jams and preserves with large fruit pieces are harder to measure accurately with a framed thermometer. Use an instant-reading thermometer with a dial that reads up to 240° F. attached to a slender metal probe for these preserves.

Be careful not to confuse a candy thermometer with a deep-fry thermometer. They are almost identical, with the difference that the deep-fry thermometer is calibrated every five degrees and the candy thermometer in two-degree increments. The more detailed

candy-making model is obviously better for preserving.

FOR SKIMMING

A fine-mesh flat sieve makes a good skimmer for removing foam from preserves as well as telltale seeds from hot marmalade. The stainless steel one I have in mind is illustrated. If you have trouble

funnel

8 oz. quilted jar

by a full 4 degrees! That difference represents from 5 to 10 minutes cooking time. It would seriously alter the consistency and taste of any finished preserve.

To compensate for a possibly faulty thermometer, each recipe in this book asks you to check its calibration. It does so by defining the jell point as a temperature eight degrees above the boiling temperature as measured on your thermometer (or 220° F. at sea level). This means you have to check your thermometer in boiling water before you use it to test preserves. This precaution is most important for cooks working above sea level whose temperature reading at the boil will, quite accurately, be lower than 212° F.

Remember to read a thermometer by bending to eye level with the top line of the column of mercury.

When using a thermometer in a hot boiling liquid, take care to submerge at least one inch of its stem without letting the tube with mercury or the metal probe touch the side or bottom of the pan. Sometimes this may require you to tip the pan toward the thermometer. Do this carefully and quickly to avoid scorching the higher end of the pot bottom. Protect the hand holding the pot from the heat with a heatproof glove.

Why the Jelly Won't Jell

Once you have visualized jelling chemistry in your mind's eye, the balance of ingredients becomes easier to predict. The higher the pectin content in a given solution, the more sugar will be needed to pluck off its water for a jell. If there is too much pectin in relation to the other ingredients, by the time the jell forms it will be tough and rubbery. It's too late to change its consistency. You'll just have to learn to love it as it is. And it will be quite flavorful.

When a recipe reaches the jell but cools to a thick, syrupy consistency, there is too much sugar in relation to the other elements. The addition of more fruit juice and a little lemon juice, as well as another short cooking period, may firm it a bit. It's really easier to use it as a syrup, in a sauce, or as an ice cream or sorbet base.

A jelly that remains thin and liquid after cooling from the jell temperature requires more cooking. Add a teaspoon of fresh lemon juice for each cup of jelly. Return the liquid to a boil and add sugar, one tablespoon at a time every minute, until the temperature rises to 222° F. Hold this temperature for a full minute before cooling the jelly again.

Jellies that weep (liquify) may contain too much acid or are being stored at too high a temperature. Pour off the excess liquid and refrigerate.

THE ARTFUL PART OF PRESERVING

Your own cooking confidence is still the most reliable testing tool in your kitchen. As you gain experience, the appearance of preserves in the pot will indicate how the preserves are cooking and when they are nearing completion. A jelly or marmalade mixture will foam up to a boil that you cannot stir down as it approaches the jell. You will have to lift the thermometer quickly to read its temperature.

finding it, use a large spoon with a shallow bowl for this job. Team up a ladle and a ½-cup bowl with a wide-mouth plastic funnel (see illustration) to fill hot jars with preserves.

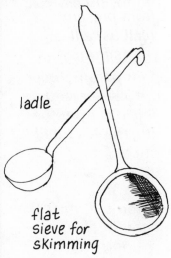

ladle

flat sieve for skimming

PARAFFIN

The paraffin used to seal the surfaces of jelly and marmalade is a waxy, solid hydrocarbon packaged in bars and commonly found in hardware or grocery stores among the canning supplies. You will melt and pour paraffin over the just-set jelly to shield it from the air. The wax will dry to form an impenetrable surface.

You will melt the paraffin after pouring jelly or marmalade. It may take 20 minutes to an hour for the jelly to set. The paraffin will melt in 5–10 minutes. Fashion a con-tainer for paraffin by bending the lip

The jams and preserves will clarify as they are nearing a jelled consistency. Rising air bubbles will become small and tightly packed. A spoon drawn across the bottom of the pan at this point will create a hissing sound. Heavy textured jams will actually begin to spit and will have to be covered when they are greatly reduced.

In recipes where the finished preserve is jelled, the amount of added sugar is determined by the fruit's pectin level. The cook's chance for personal expression is a matter of selecting tasty fruit combinations, such as pairing sweet with sour, and using seasonings imaginatively. When making jams where pectin is not an issue, all the ingredients may be varied.

But just how does one go about experimenting with new seasonings? You could begin by simply substituting one herb for another. If basil makes a fragrant flavor, why not try the highly aromatic marjoram or tarragon in that recipe? Or introduce the gentle fragrance of a cinnamon stick to a preserve that lacks any other seasoning. For a more adventuresome leap, add an assertive spice like cardamom seed that works well in one recipe to season another similarly flavored fruit. I added cardamom to Red Currant Jelly (see index) because currants have a slightly astringent taste, much like that in the sour skin of plum, a fruit that cardamom compliments very well.

How can one anticipate the room temperature taste of a boiling hot preserve? You will have to cool down a small amount of preserves to detect the flavor relationships. The tastes of sweetness, sourness, and warmth overwhelm our sensors when we sample a hot jam or jelly. Spice and herb aromatics will permeate our nose. Only when it is cooled to room temperature do the floral aromas of fruit develop and balance these other sensations.

HOW TO COMPLETE THE PRESERVING PROCESS

Each recipe in the book includes a compact guide to sealing, processing, and storing your preserves. Let's run through this part of the preserving process step by step for both wax-sealed and vacuum-sealed jars.

1. Wash, rinse, submerge, boil, and drain jars (explained on page 15).

2. When the fruits are cooked to their proper temperature or consistency, take the pot off the heat. Skim off any foam or pips (seeds). Remove the sterilized jars from the pot and set them upside down on a rack to dry for two to three minutes. This brief rest for the preserves will allow them to cool slightly. This is advisable particularly for marmalade and preserves. If these jell a bit, the fruit pieces will remain more evenly distributed in the jars after they are poured.

You may also want to spend this brief period checking your yield against that stated in the recipe. Ladle the preserve into a one-quart glass measure that has been rinsed in boiling water.

3. Sterilize the lids (see page 16).

4. Fit the funnel into the mouth of each hot, dry jar (see illustration on page 29) and prepare to ladle in the hot preserves. If you are working with marmalade, stir it gently to redistribute the peels. Since marmalade and jelly will be sealed with paraffin, fill them to

paraffin pitcher

of an empty one-pound shortening or coffee tin into a spout (see illustration above). Break a bar of paraffin into it and set the can in a larger saucepan filled with one inch of water. Heat the water in the saucepan to a boil, then turn off the heat. The paraffin will slowly melt in its can as the surrounding hot water warms it.

This hot water bath keeps the melted paraffin liquid for a while.

The bath also protects this highly flammable hydrocarbon from direct contact with heat. This homemade paraffin pitcher will become a permanent part of your preserving equipment.

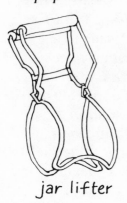

jar lifter

It's also important to have a heavy-duty lifter for moving the filled and processed jars in and out of the boiling water bath

within ½ inch of the rim. Cover the jars with plastic wrap to protect them from contact with the air for a few minutes until their tops have set. Wipe clean the inside of the rim down to the jelly with a damp cloth that has been dipped in boiling water and pour a ⅛-inch layer of melted paraffin on the top. Rotate each jar at a slight angle to drive the wax up the sides of the jar and seal the edges. Cool the jars to room temperature on a rack.

The jam and preserves are a bit more fragile because of their higher moisture content. To be absolutely certain that there is no air in the jar that could support bacteria, these products will have to be tightly sealed. First fill jam and preserve jars to within ⅛-inch of the lip. Check the rim of each jar to see that it is clean before attaching a dry lid. If you see drops of water or jam, wipe it clean with a cloth dipped first in boiling water and then wrung dry. Screw the cap on tightly and follow up with a vacuum sealing process. Either invert each jar briefly or submerge them by one inch in a boiling water bath for 10 minutes. I suggest you use the more thorough water bath to process the no-sugar jams since they have no sucrose (refined sugar) to protect them from spoiling.

STORING PRESERVES

Preserves should cool to room temperature overnight on a rack. The best storage place is in a dry, dark cellar with a temperature range of 50-60° F. *Discard any product that develops mold, a fermented odor, or changed appearance during storage.* It was once common practice simply to scrape the mold off the top of jelly and eat what lay underneath. We now know that these molds can produce deep, invisible roots that carry mycotoxins which can build up in the body over time. Also be sure to refrigerate your preserves after opening, for they are vulnerable at room temperature once their seal is broken.

But don't hoard them! Your jams and jellies will always taste better if eaten within four months of preserving. They also make wonderful gifts. You can easily dress them up with a square of cotton gingham tied over the lids and a decorative label. Voilà! You've got a product as pretty as any store-bought gourmet item—one that delivers a fresh fruit taste of great integrity.

(see illustration on page 30).

The main concern in carefully processing preserves is simply to protect your work from spoiling before you have the chance to enjoy it.

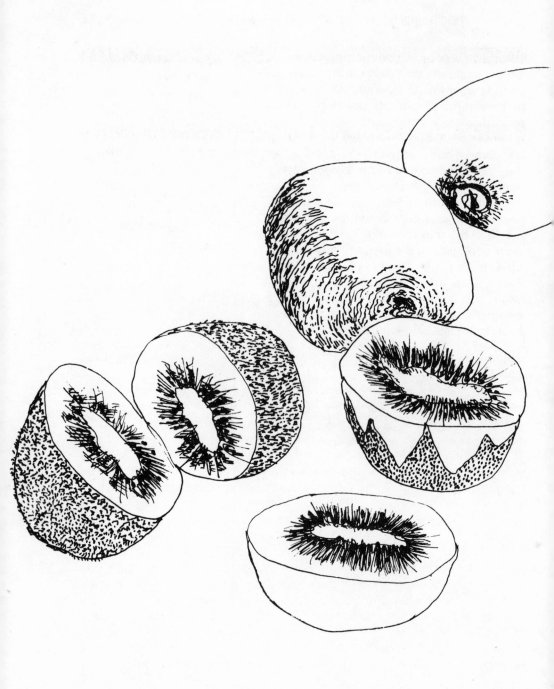

3

JAMS

Fruit jam is the easiest medium in which beginning preservers can work. It is simply sweet, concentrated fruit pulp. The cook has more control over ingredient proportions and technique here than in any of the other preserving methods.

Each jam recipe in this chapter begins with directions for cutting up the fresh fruit. Pineapple, for example, is cut into narrow wedges one time and coarsely chopped another. Pears are diced in one recipe and thinly sliced in another. As each pound of fruit or berries cooks and reduces (to about 1 cup of pulp and concentrated juices), these initial shapes will affect the jam's texture and, ultimately, its feel in the mouth. As you gain experience in making preserves, you will learn to recognize the characteristic crunch of slender apple slices and the slippery feel of pineapple strands on the tongue as physical sensations essential to the taste of jam. Think about the textural potential of the fruits as you prepare them for cooking. You can easily plan the effect you want them to make.

Another way to affect jam texture is by shortening or lengthening the cooking time. You may prefer a loose jam consistency to one that is thicker and stiffer. The longer the cooking, the denser the jam.

Because the thickness of a jam results from reduction rather than from jelling, the amount of sugar added to the pot can also be altered. Sweet or bland fruit ingredients may call for as little as ¼ cup sugar per cup of reduced fruit. Blueberries, for example, need minimal sweetening and cooking to offer fresh-air fragrance and soft texture. A tart fruit, such as rhubarb, by contrast, will take a cup or more sugar to sweeten the same volume. I have tried to make sure that sugar flatters the fruit without dominating the taste in all these recipes.

The introduction of herbs, spices, lemon juice, or liqueur adds new interest and depth to fruit flavors. The scent of mint in one blueberry jam heightens its cool, refreshing effect. Likewise, the heat of crystallized ginger pieces in the mouth verifies and intensifies the sweet-sour taste in Rhubarb Ginger Jam (see index).

How does the preserver combine technique with all this variability to come up with optimum results? The key is efficient timing along with artful balance of a jam's tastes, textures, and scents. I have tried to ensure consistently excellent results by giving specific weights and measures of ingredients and exact cooking times in these recipes. If you observe these guidelines when you begin preserving, you will build cooking skills that you can later apply to your own experiments.

If you wish to develop a jam flavor of your own, be prepared for some trial and error. A preserve tastes considerably different hot than it does after it has cooled. When a jam is hot, sweet and sour tastes are accentuated, and these can overwhelm the aroma of the fruit and some seasonings. Preserves have to cool and often sit a day or two before fruit flavor and aroma fully bloom.

You can adjust and balance jam flavor by taking the pot off the heat to check it. Transfer a tablespoon of hot jam from the pot to a small dish and cool it quickly in the freezer until it reaches room temperature. Taste it and make whatever additions you desire based on this cooled sample of the jam. A brief interruption in the reducing process will not compromise the quality of the preserve.

TECHNIQUE FOR MAKING JAMS

Let's examine the step-by-step technique for making jams.

1. Each recipe tells you how to cut up or otherwise prepare the fruit, what pot to use, and how to combine the fruits called for.

2. Some sugar is added at the beginning of the cooking process in many of the recipes to draw out the moisture in the fruit and provide a liquid in which to cook the fruit. When the sugar volume is small in the recipe, water often replaces sugar for this preliminary cooking.

3. The heat must be medium-low under the fruit until there is enough juice to come to a simmer. At this point the fruit is covered and cooked

slowly for a short time to soften the fruit and draw out juices with a minimum of evaporation. You should lift the lid every two to three minutes to check and see that the simmer is slow and leisurely.

4. Once the fruit is surrounded by or floating in liquid, the pot lid comes off and the heat is turned up to medium. You then add sugar, ½ cup at a time, waiting for the jam to return to the boil before adding more.

As some of these jams thicken, they may sputter and spit hot liquids. I will alert you to this possibility in the recipe. You will partly cover the pot and stir it off the heat every minute or two. In fact, it's a good policy always to have a lid at hand to contain any unexpected spatters from the pot.

5. After all the sugar is added, the jam is cooked until it reaches a specific temperature. When a jam is quite thick and a thermometer will not be able to give an accurate reading, the recipe will call for the spoon test. If liquid falls from the bowl of a metal spoon in a single sheet rather than in isolated drops, the jam is done (illustrated on page 24).

Most recipes give both the length of cooking time after all the sugar is added and a total cooking time for the whole recipe so you can verify your work as you cook. A final jam volume is also given should you want to evaluate your work that way.

6. Each recipe ends with specific directions for processing the jams in the jars so they seal properly. Use quilted preserving jars with vacuum-sealable lids and screw caps for all jams. You can either invert the newly filled jars to seal them or process them in a boiling water bath. If you are not sure of the water bath procedure, review the detailed account of this technique in Chapter 2 on preserving equipment.

Apple Ginger Jam

Not to be confused with applesauce, this soft preserve contains firm apple bits and chewy fragments of peel. The addition of tart lemon juice and tingling ginger root slices guarantees a good balance of sweet, sour, and spicy sensations.

This jam would taste great on Apple Cinnamon Muffins or Butter-milk Currant Scones (see index for recipes). You could easily use it to make an Apple Jam Tart garnished with fresh apple slices or freeze it using the Philadelphia-style Ice Cream recipe (see index for recipes). Wouldn't creamy apple ginger ice cream served with a warm burnt caramel sauce make a wonderful dessert?

1 cup water
½ tablespoon fresh lemon juice
3 pounds apples (use half Granny Smith, half MacIntosh)
2½ cups sugar
3 slices fresh ginger (size of a quarter)
Zest of 1 lemon

Combine water and lemon juice in a heavy, nonreactive 4-quart pot.

Quarter and core the apples but leave on the skins. Dice apples and immediately toss them in the acidulated water. (If you are using a food processor, place quarters of 2 apples at a time in the workbowl fitted with a steel blade and chop into small pieces with rapid on-and-off motions.)

Stir 1 cup sugar and the ginger slices in with the apples and bring this mixture to a boil. Reduce the heat and simmer, uncovered, for 10 minutes.

Begin adding the remaining 1½ cups sugar, ½ cup at a time. Stir in thin strips of lemon peel removed with a zester. Lower the heat as the jam thickens and cook another 5 minutes.

Off the heat, remove the ginger slices. Spoon the apple jam into hot, sterilized jars to within ⅛ inch of the lips. Wipe rims clean, attach new lids, and screw caps on tightly. Invert the jars briefly for a quick vacuum seal or process in a boiling water bath, submerged by 1 inch of water, for 10 minutes.

YIELD: 5 cups

Ginger Pear Jam

A supply of knobby fresh ginger root is indispensable to fine fruit preserving. This seasoning generates a surge of warmth on the tongue and a spicy fragrance that enhances the delicate floral aroma and taste of pears and many other fruits. Here, as elsewhere, the lemon juice adds just enough acid to balance the flavor of other ingredients.

Savor the pleasures of this taste-tingling jam on Risen Biscuits or warm Cream Scones (see index).

3 pounds Bartlett pears
1 tablespoon fresh lemon juice
1 cup sugar
2 slices fresh ginger root (size of a quarter)

Peel, quarter, and core the pears. Coarsely chop them. Combine pears in a heavy, nonreactive 4-quart pan with lemon juice, ½ cup sugar, and ginger slices.

Bring mixture to a boil, regulate to a simmer, and cook for 15 minutes, partially covered. Stir every 3-5 minutes.

Add remaining ½ cup sugar and continue cooking, uncovered, for another 10 minutes, stirring every 2-3 minutes. (After 10 minutes the jam will have thickened noticeably and reduced to about 3 cups.)

Remove the ginger slices and fill hot, sterilized jars to within ⅛ inch of lips. Wipe rims clean, attach new lids, and screw caps on tightly. Invert jars briefly for a quick vacuum seal or process in a boiling water bath, submerged by 1 inch, for 10 minutes.

YIELD: 3 cups

Pear and Pineapple Jam

The pear and pineapple, so different in taste and texture, make a wonderfully harmonious preserve that blends their flavors but respects the consistency and scent of each.

A plateful of Oatmeal Muffins or Drop Scones (see index) would complement this jam well.

2 pounds Bartlett pears
2½ pounds pineapple (1 pound peeled and cored)
½ cup water
½ tablespoon fresh lemon juice
1 cup sugar
Zest from 1 lemon

Peel, quarter, and core pears. Cut pears and pineapple into pieces the size of lima beans. (If you are using a food processor, cut each fruit separately with the steel blade, making rapid on-and-off motions.)

Combine fruits with water and lemon juice in a heavy, nonreactive 4-quart pan. Bring the water to a boil, adjust heat to a slow simmer, cover, and cook for 15 minutes. Stir every 5 minutes.

Add sugar ½ cup at a time and boil another 10 minutes, stirring frequently to prevent sticking. An instant-reading thermometer will rise to 212-214°F. as the jam reduces to 3½ cups. Off heat, stir in the lemon zest removed with a zester (illustrated in Chapter 2).

Fill hot, sterilized jars to within ⅛ inch of lips. Wipe rims clean, attach new lids, and screw on the caps tightly. Invert briefly for a quick vacuum seal or process in a boiling water bath, submerged by 1 inch, for 10 minutes.

YIELD: 3½ cups

Pear and Plum Jam

Although they rarely appear together, pears and plums are quite compatible fruits. This recipe offers a quick and easy way to preserve their summer-fresh flavors and aromas for cold weather breakfasts or tea served with English Muffins or Grapenuts Muffins (see index).

2 pounds Bartlett pears
1½ pounds Italian plums
1 cup sugar
1 tablespoon fresh lemon juice

Peel, core, and quarter pears. Halve and pit the plums. Chop fruits into ½-inch pieces. (If you are using a machine for this job, process each fruit separately with rapid on-and-off motions, using the steel blade.)

Bring fruit pieces to a boil with the sugar and the lemon juice in a heavy, nonreactive 5-quart pan. Regulate the heat to simmer slowly, partially cover the pan, and cook for up to 30 minutes. Stir at least once every 5 minutes to check for sticking.

Jam is done when there is little standing liquid on top of the fruit pulp and bubbles heave mightily with a noisy plopping sound.

Fill hot, sterilized jars to within ⅛ inch of the lips. Wipe rims clean, attach new lids, and screw the caps on tightly. Invert the jars briefly for a quick vacuum seal or process in a boiling water bath, submerged by 1 inch, for 10 minutes.

YIELD: 4½ cups

Red Raspberry Jam

This is a favorite jam of mine, and one of the easiest to make. The only trick is finding fresh red currants. Although you could substitute sieved red or black raspberry juice with delicious results, it is worthwhile to search out the currants. The two fruits together offer an intensely interesting flavor.

This jam is delicious with all the breads. My favorites are the Buttermilk Currant Scones and Tea Brack (see index).

2 cups red currant juice (strained from 2½ pounds red currants)
2 pounds red raspberries
5½ cups sugar

Bake red currants, stems on, in a heavy, nonreactive 5-quart covered pot in a preheated 350° F. oven for 40 minutes. Strain the berries for 3 hours or overnight and discard the fruit pieces. If there is more than 2 cups juice, reduce it. If there is less than 2 cups, augment the juice with enough red raspberries to make 2 cups.

Warm the sugar in a 250° F. oven for 10 minutes.

Combine raspberries and juice in a 4-quart saucepan and bring to a boil. Simmer 5 minutes.

Begin adding sugar ½ cup at a time. Stir it in and wait until jam returns to the boil before adding more. Cook mixture to the jell point, which is 8 degrees above the boiling temperature on your thermometer, stirring frequently to prevent sticking. (Allow as much as 15 minutes of cooking time after sugar is added.)

Fill hot, sterilized jars to within ⅛ inch of lips. Wipe the rims clean, attach new lids, and screw caps on tightly. Invert jars for a quick seal or process in a boiling water bath, submerged by 1 inch, for 10 minutes.

YIELD: 6 cups

Raspberry Pear Jam

Red raspberries and pears make a dynamic pair that taste wonderful served fresh or cooked, hot or cold.

This jam is delicious spread on a warm English Muffin or Cream Scone (see index).

1 pound Bartlett pears
1½ pounds red raspberries
2 cups sugar

Peel, quarter, and core the pears. Dice them finely and toss them in a heavy, nonreactive 4-quart pan with the red raspberries and 1 cup sugar. Heat the pot until the sugar melts, reduce heat to a gentle simmer, cover, and cook the fruits for 10 minutes. Lift the lid every 3 minutes to check the simmer and stir.

Add ½ cup sugar and continue cooking at a steady simmer, uncovered, for 5 minutes. Stir in the remaining ½ cup sugar and cook another 2-3 minutes.

Partly cover the pot to prevent spattering when necessary. Also stir frequently to prevent sticking. A finished temperature reading is 212° F. Total cooking time will be about 18 minutes. Jam will reduce to a quart.

Off heat, pour jam into hot, sterilized jars to within ⅛ inch of the lip. Wipe rims clean, attach new lids, and screw the caps on tightly. Invert the jars briefly for a quick vacuum seal or process in a boiling water bath, submerged by 1 inch, for 10 minutes.

YIELD: 4 cups

Double Black Raspberry Jam

The concentrated essence of wild black raspberries in this jam recalls the cool, damp air trapped in wooded raspberry thickets on hot afternoons in early July.

2 cups sieved black raspberries (purée of 2 pints berries)
2½ cups sugar
1 pound whole black raspberries
1 tablespoon fresh lemon juice

Use a sieve or food mill to separate the juices and pulp of the raspberries from the seeds. Simmer the raspberry purée that results with 1 cup sugar over low heat for 10 minutes in a heavy, nonreactive 4-quart pot. Stir frequently. Stir in the whole berries and cook over medium-low heat another 10 minutes.

Add the remaining 1½ cups sugar, ½ cup at a time, and the lemon juice. Cook over medium-high heat, now stirring constantly, until jam reaches 216-218° F. This should happen in 7-10 minutes.

Fill hot, sterilized jars to within ⅛ inch of the lips. Wipe the rims clean, attach new lids, and screw caps on tightly. Seal by quickly inverting the jars or process in a boiling water bath, submerged by 1 inch, for 10 minutes.

YIELD: 3 cups

Cherry and Red Raspberry Jam

The red raspberries in this jam accentuate the fragile flavor of the cherries, which usually dissipates when cherries are cooked and sweetened.

I serve this jam on special occasions and give it as gifts to friends. It is terrific on Butter Pecan Muffins, Cream Scones, and English Muffins (see index).

2 pounds pitted sour cherries (generally available—in season—at fruitstands, orchards, and farmers' markets)
1 pound red raspberries
2 cups sugar

Combine fruits in a heavy, nonreactive 4-quart pot and bring to a boil. Simmer 20 minutes, stirring regularly. The mixture will thicken but should not stick.

Begin adding sugar ½ cup at a time, stirring frequently. Let the jam cook up to 10 minutes more. It should be noticeably thickened with a temperature reading of about 215-216°F.

Off heat, skim and fill hot, sterilized jars to within ⅛ inch of lips. Wipe the rims clean, attach new lids, and screw caps on tightly. Invert the jars for a quick seal or process in a boiling water bath, submerged by 1 inch, for 10 minutes.

YIELD: 4½ cups

Rhubarb Ginger Jam

Rhubarb jam with ginger was one of the first fruit preserves I ever made. I was thrilled with its dramatic balance of tart rhubarb, hot ginger, and sweet sugar.

I recommend you first try this jam on chewy English Muffins (see index) so you can fully enjoy the feel of clusters of rhubarb strands and exciting hot tiny bits of crystallized ginger.

2 pounds fresh or frozen dry-pack rhubarb
8 3-inch strips lemon peel (approximately ¼ inch wide)
2 fresh ginger root slices (size of a quarter)
½ cup water
2½ cups sugar
2 ounces (⅓ cup) thinly sliced crystallized ginger

Rinse, trim, and cut fresh rhubarb stalks into ½-inch lengths. Combine with lemon strips (removed with a stripper, which is illustrated in Chapter 2), ginger root slices, and water in a heavy, nonreactive 4-quart pan. Bring water to a boil, slow it to a simmer, cover, and gently cook for 30 minutes. Lift lid and stir every 5 minutes.

Remove ginger root slices, turn up the heat, and begin adding sugar ½ cup at a time, waiting for the liquid to return to the boil before adding more. Continue cooking over high heat, stirring constantly, until the jam thickens and reduces to about 3 cups. Stir in the crystallized ginger pieces at the end of the cooking period.

Off heat, skim and fill hot, sterilized jars to within ⅛ inch of lips. Wipe rims clean, attach new lids, and screw caps on tightly. Invert jars briefly for a quick vacuum seal or process in a boiling water bath, submerged by 1 inch, for 10 minutes.

YIELD: 3 cups

Rhubarb Blackberry Jam

Since fresh rhubarb and blackberries are not available at the market at the same time, you will have to supply your own from the garden or substitute a frozen product for one of the fruits. Let the frozen fruit come almost to room temperature before starting the recipe. The frozen fruit will exude more liquid than fresh and may require a slightly longer cooking time.

Serve this jam with any one of the chewy English Muffin recipes (see index).

¾ pound rhubarb
1 pound fresh or frozen blackberries
½ cup water
1¾ cups sugar

Rinse and trim rhubarb. Cut into ½-inch lengths.

Combine rhubarb and blackberries with water in a heavy, nonreactive 5-quart pan. Bring to a boil and simmer, covered, for 10 minutes until the fruits soften and release juice but remain whole.

Begin adding sugar ½ cup at a time, returning the liquid to the boil before adding more. Stir jam continuously until it thickens noticeably and the bubble pattern is quite dense. Temperature of jam should be 210° F.

Fill hot, sterilized jars to within ⅛ inch of lips. Wipe off rims, attach new lids, and screw caps on tightly. Invert briefly for a quick vacuum seal or process in a boiling water bath, submerged by 1 inch, for 10 minutes.

YIELD: 3 cups

Apricot Blueberry Jam

The cooking time for this jam is short, and little sugar is added, so the generous yield of soft, reduced fruit pieces is intensely fresh-tasting.

This jam is delicious served with Zucchini Bread or Grapenuts Muffins (see index).

2 pounds apricots (4 cups after peeling and pitting)
1 cup sugar
1 pound blueberries

Dip the apricots in boiling water for 30 seconds. Remove them and cool under running water. Slip off their skins, remove pits, and slice apricots. Combine them with ½ cup sugar in a heavy, nonreactive 4-quart pot. Simmer and stir frequently for 10 minutes. Add the remaining ½ cup sugar and cook 5 minutes more. (Mixture will thicken and may begin to spit. When this begins, partially cover the pot but continue to stir frequently.)

Stir in the blueberries and simmer for 5 minutes. Give the jam the cold plate test at this point. Chill a tablespoon of the mixture on a cold plate. If it holds its shape, it has thickened enough. If it is too soft and wet, cook another 2 minutes and test again. The temperature of the jam will rise as high as 206° F.

Off the heat, skim off foam. Pour the jam into hot, sterilized jars to within ⅛ inch of the lips. Wipe the rims clean, attach new lids, and screw the caps on tightly. Invert the jars briefly for a quick vacuum seal or process in a boiling water bath, submerged by 1 inch, for 10 minutes.

YIELD: 5½ cups

Apricot Orange Jam

The acidic bite of orange juice and its fresh citrus scent accentuate the perfumed sweetness in apricots. Together they make a sunny, light preserve that is perfect for a brunch buffet, spread on freshly baked Risen Biscuits or Cornmeal Muffins (see index).

2 pounds ripe apricots, skins removed, pitted, and thinly sliced (4 cups)
1 6-ounce can unsweetened orange juice concentrate
¾ cup water
1¼ cups sugar
Zest of 1 orange
¼ cup apricot liqueur

Combine apricot slices with concentrate and water in a heavy, nonreactive 5-quart pan. Bring to a simmer and cook slowly for 10 minutes, stirring regularly. (Apricot slices will cook and soften. As the mixture thickens bubbles will become small and tightly packed. Portions of it will begin to heave and plop.)

Stir in sugar ½ cup at a time, then add the last ¼ cup and the zest, removed with a zester (illustrated in Chapter 2). Continue to stir and simmer on low for 10 minutes. Add liqueur and cook another 2 minutes to thicken jam a bit more. Stir continuously at this point to prevent sticking. Jam should pass the spoon test (a tablespoon of jam will fall from a metal spoon in a single stream rather than in isolated drops). The candy thermometer will rise to 200°F.

Fill hot, sterilized jars to within ⅛ inch of lips. Wipe the rims clean, attach new lids, and screw caps on tightly. Vacuum seal by inverting quickly or process in a boiling water bath, submerged by 1 inch, for 10 minutes.

YIELD: 3 cups

Peach and Blueberry Jam

A jam made with sliced peaches and blueberries retains fresh and delicate fruit flavors when it is cooked briefly and gently.

Enjoy the subtlety of this jam with Cream Scones, Risen Biscuits, or Oatmeal Muffins (see index).

2 pounds peaches, peeled, pitted, and thinly sliced (3 cups)
3 cups sugar
1 pound blueberries

Combine peach slices and sugar in a deep, nonreactive 5-quart saucepan. Bring to a boil and cook over medium heat, stirring constantly, for 10-15 minutes. (Judge the cooking time by looking at and listening to the peach mixture. It will be thick with bubbles. The pot will make a hissing sound as you pull the spoon across the bottom, but the peach pulp will not stick.)

Lower the heat, add the blueberries, cover, and simmer slowly for 5 minutes. Uncover the pot, turn up the heat, and begin cooking vigorously again, stirring constantly. In 5 minutes or so the jam should be thickened. A thermometer reading at this point will be 210° F.

Fill hot, sterilized jars to within ⅛ inch of lips. Wipe the rims clean, attach new lids, and screw caps on tightly. Invert jars for a quick vacuum seal or process jars in a boiling water bath, submerged by 1 inch, for 10 minutes.

YIELD: 3½ cups

Kiwifruit Pineapple Jam

Kiwifruit is a newcomer to preserving. Originally a native of New Zealand, kiwifruit is now grown in California and available throughout the year, at more reasonable prices. Its acid green color and tiny black seeds are quite dramatic but fade as you cook it, so I always add some fruit just at the end of the cooking process.

The pineapple and kiwifruit have similar flavor profiles. They are lusciously sweet when ripe but acidic to the point of astringency before that. The sugar you add will temper the fruit acid and allow their distinct and complementary tastes to mingle.

Warm Risen Biscuits and Cream Scones (see index) taste wonderful with this jam.

6 large kiwifruits, cut into wedges (3 cups)
1 pound 10 ounces peeled, cored, and chopped fresh pineapple (4 cups)
3 cups sugar

Peel and quarter kiwifruits lengthwise. Cut them into thin pie-shaped wedges. (If using a food processor, chop 3 kiwi fruits at a time, quartered, with rapid on and off motions, until they are ½-inch bits.)

Cut each pineapple quarter lengthwise into 6 sections, then crosswise into wedges. (Cut pieces into a uniform size and process ½ the pieces at a time with rapid on and off motions in the food processor.)

Combine all the pineapple and 2 cups kiwifruit pieces in a heavy, nonreactive 4-quart pan. Reserve remaining kiwifruit (about 1 cup).

Bring fruits to a boil with 1 cup sugar. Reduce heat to a gentle simmer, cover the pot, and simmer for 10 minutes. Uncover the pan, turn up heat to medium-high, and vigorously simmer the fruit for 5 minutes, stirring regularly.

Begin adding the remaining sugar ½ cup at a time. Continue to boil for 10 more minutes or until the jam reaches 216° F. and passes the spoon test. To make the spoon test, raise a metal spoon filled with the hot jam above the pot and empty it from the side. If jam falls from the spoon in a single sheet rather than in isolated drops, the jam has reached 216° F. (illustrated on page 24).

Off the heat, stir in the remaining pieces of kiwifruit. Boil jam until it thickens again and the temperature returns to 216° F. This will take another 5 minutes.

Off the heat, skim foam from the surface and fill hot, sterilized jars to within ⅛ inch of lips. Wipe the rims clean, attach new lids, and screw caps on tightly. Invert jars for a quick vacuum seal or process in a boiling water bath, submerged by 1 inch, for 10 minutes.

YIELD: 3½ cups

Kiwifruit Mint Jam

A touch of citrus fragrance and the cool, soothing sensation of fresh mint in this kiwifruit jam highlight the considerable flavor range in this fuzzy little fruit. It is sweet, a bit acidic, particularly before it ripens, and its scent recalls ripe bananas and strawberries. Savor the subtlety of this jam spread on English Muffins or a Cream Scone (see index).

2 pounds ripe kiwifruit
Zest of 1 lemon
2 cups sugar
3 6-inch sprigs fresh mint

Peel and quarter kiwifruit. Slice thinly and combine with lemon zest removed with a zester (illustrated in Chapter 2) in a heavy, nonreactive 4-quart pan. Bring fruit to a boil, reduce heat to a simmer, and cook for 10 minutes, stirring every 2-3 minutes.

When the mixture hisses as a spoon is drawn through it, begin adding the sugar ½ cup at a time. Continue cooking briskly and stirring until jam mixture thickens and there is a tight pattern of bubbles over the top. This will happen in less than 5 minutes. The temperature of the hot liquid will be 212° F.

Off the heat, crush the mint sprigs in the hot jam. Let them steep for 2 minutes. Cool a spoonful of jam and taste. Remove the stems when the taste of mint is noticeable but before it is pronounced.

Fill hot, sterilized jars to within ⅛ inch of lips. Wipe the rims clean, attach new lids, and screw caps on tightly. Invert jars briefly for a quick vacuum seal or process in a boiling water bath, submerged by 1 inch, for 10 minutes.

YIELD: 2⅔ cups

Nectarine Slices with Grand Marnier

The nectarine is a variety of peach with a fine flavor and good acidity. Pectin stock is added here to help hold the slippery fruit slices in their fragrant juices. Try it with Grapenuts Muffins or Butter Pecan Muffins (see index).

3 pounds ripe nectarines (12 medium)
¾ cup water
1⅓ cups Pectin Stock (see index)
3 cups sugar
½ cup Grand Marnier liqueur

Submerge the nectarines for 1 minute in boiling water, cool them under running water, and peel. Pit and thinly slice them. There will be about 7 cups fruit.

Combine slices with water in a heavy, nonreactive 4-quart saucepan and cook over medium-low heat for 15 minutes, stirring frequently to prevent sticking.

Pour in the Pectin Stock and return jam to a simmer. Stir in the sugar ½ cup at a time, returning liquid to a simmer before adding more. Stir constantly for 10-15 minutes as the jam thickens. When temperature is around 215° F., pour in the Grand Marnier. Cook another 2 minutes.

Fill hot, sterilized jars to within ⅛ inch of lips. Wipe the rims clean, attach new lids, and screw caps on tightly. Invert jars for a quick seal or process in a boiling water bath, submerged by 1 inch, for 10 minutes.

YIELD: 4½ cups

Pineapple Blueberry Jam

A jam of pineapple and blueberries is bound to contain rich contrasts in taste, texture, and scent.

A fresh, warm plateful of English Muffins (see index) and cold sweet butter for sampling it are definitely in order.

3 pounds ripe pineapple (1¼ pounds peeled and cored)
1½ cups sugar
1½ tablespoons fresh lime juice
1 pound fresh blueberries

Quarter the peeled pineapple. Remove the core segment and slice lengthwise into 5 or 6 pieces. Cut across these slices to make thin wedge-shaped pieces.

Bring pineapple pieces to a boil in a heavy, nonreactive 5-quart pot. Reduce heat to a simmer and cook, covered, for 15 minutes. Take off pot lid, turn up the heat to medium, and reduce the pineapple juices for 10 minutes or until almost dry.

Combine 1 cup sugar and 1 tablespoon lime juice with the pineapple. Bring to a boil and cook to 220° F. in about 5-10 minutes.

Off the heat, stir in the blueberries, the remaining ½ cup sugar, and the remaining ½ tablespoon lime juice. Cook the jam over medium-high heat for another 10-15 minutes. Regularly shake the pot and scrape the bottom of the pan with a spatula to check for sticking. Otherwise, do not stir the pot. Jam is ready when liquids pass the spoon test. When a metal spoonful of jam is tipped, the liquid should fall in a single sheet rather than in separate drops (illustrated on page 24). A thermometer will rise to 210° F.

Fill hot, sterilized jars to within ⅛ inch of the lips. Wipe rims clean, attach new lids, and screw caps on tightly. Invert jars for a quick seal, or process in a boiling water bath, submerged by 1 inch, for 10 minutes.

YIELD: 3 cups

Tomato Prune Jam

This recipe is for the more adventuresome eater who seeks out new taste experiences. Tomatoes and prunes make quite a mild, sweet blend; the red wine vinegar added at the very end contrasts and accentuates the ingredients.

This soft, spreadable jam is great on warm Oatmeal Muffins and Buttermilk Currant Scones (see index).

12 ounces pitted prunes
2 pounds ripe tomatoes (4-5 medium)
Bouquet garni: 1 cinnamon stick, 3 cloves, 3 allspice berries,
        2 lemon peel strips
½ cup granulated sugar
½ cup brown sugar
1 tablespoon (or more to taste) red wine vinegar

Cut prunes into small pieces. Dip the tomatoes in simmering water for 30 seconds. Cool under running water and peel them. Core and quarter the tomatoes. Force out seeds into a fine strainer and reserve the juices. Coarsely chop tomato pieces.

Combine prunes, tomatoes, strained juices, and *bouquet garni* in a deep, nonreactive 4-quart saucepan. Bring to a simmer and cook at an active simmer, uncovered, for 15 minutes, stirring regularly. (The mixture will thicken and be free of standing liquid.)

Stir in the sugars one at a time. Continue cooking for another 10 minutes until the jam is thick again and a thermometer reads 208-210° F.

Off the heat, remove the bouquet, and stir in the vinegar. Quickly cool a tablespoon of jam in the freezer and taste for the slightly tart finish of the vinegar to balance the sweet fruits. Add more vinegar if desired.

Fill hot, sterilized jars to within ⅛ inch of the lips. Wipe the rims clean, attach new lids, and screw caps on tightly. Process in a boiling water bath, submerged by 1 inch, for 10 minutes. Alternatively, quick-seal by inverting the hot jam in the freshly packed jar.

YIELD: 4 cups

Tomato Basil Jam

I could not resist the desire to bring the synergetic team of tomato and basil into this collection. Balance is important here. You will want to cool and taste this jam carefully to bring sweet and sour elements into equilibrium. Add the remaining basil strips as the jam cools so they retain their vivid green color.

This jam is quite good with Risen Biscuits and Whole Wheat English Muffins (see index).

3 pounds ripe tomatoes
2 lemons
1 cup sugar
24 fresh basil leaves

Dip the tomatoes in simmering water for 30 seconds. Cool them under running water. Peel, core, quarter, and coarsely chop them. They will measure a generous 4 cups.

Cook tomatoes at an active simmer in a deep, nonreactive 4-quart pan for 30 minutes or until they are reduced to between 2½ and 3 cups.

While the tomatoes cook, remove the yellow zest from the 2 lemons with a zester (illustrated in Chapter 2). Squeeze the juice from both lemons. Purée 12 basil leaves in the lemon juice.

Off the heat, stir the zest and the sugar into the tomatoes. Return the tomato mixture to a simmer and cook, stirring frequently, for 10 minutes, until the jam thickens again. The thermometer reading will be 210° F.

Off the heat, stir in 5 tablespoons of lemon basil juice. Freeze a tablespoon of jam briefly. When cooled to room temperature, taste for a balance of sweet and sour. Add more lemon juice by the tablespoon as needed.

Cut the remaining basil leaves into thin strips. Fold them into the jam.

Fill hot, sterilized jars to within ⅛ inch of the lips. Wipe rims clean, attach new lids, and screw caps on tightly. Invert the jars quickly to force out the air for a quick seal or process them in a boiling water bath, submerged by 1 inch, for 10 minutes.

YIELD: 2½–3 cups

Tomato Orange Jam

This jam celebrates my favorite winter lunch drink, a mug of hot V-8 juice flavored with a little orange juice and scented with spices. It's a taste combination that works beautifully in a preserve with fresh tomatoes.

You can warm the jam if you like by eating it on oven-fresh Cornmeal Muffins (see index).

3 pounds ripe tomatoes
2 navel oranges
***Bouquet garni:* 3 cloves, 3 allspice berries, 1 slice fresh ginger**
1 cup sugar
2 tablespoons unsweetened orange juice concentrate (optional)
Tomato paste (optional)

Submerge tomatoes in boiling water for 30 seconds. Cool under running water. Peel, core, and quarter. Force out seeds and liquid through a sieve; coarsely chop the pulp. Tomato pieces and strained juices will measure about 4 cups.

Remove the zest from both oranges with a zester (illustrated in Chapter 2). Cut away and discard inner white peel. Halve the oranges, remove seeds, and thinly slice.

Place tomatoes, orange zest, orange slices, and the *bouquet garni* in a deep, nonreactive 4-quart saucepan. Cook this mixture at an active simmer for 25-30 minutes until the mixture has reduced to 3 cups.

Stir in sugar ½ cup at a time, allowing the jam to return to the simmer between additions. Cook at a simmer for another 10 minutes until reduced again to about 3 cups. Temperature of mixture will reach 210° F.

Off the heat, remove *bouquet garni*. Cool a tablespoon of jam in the freezer and taste for an even blend of tomato and orange flavors. Add orange juice concentrate or a little tomato paste as needed for balance.

Fill hot, sterilized jars to within ⅛ inch of the lips. Wipe rims clean, attach new lids, and screw caps on tightly. Invert jars to quick-seal or process in a boiling water bath, submerged by 1 inch, for 10 minutes.

YIELD: almost 3 cups

Rhubarb Fig Jam

Bits of dried figs remain intact in this jam and leave nuggets of pure sweetness scattered throughout the tangy rhubarb strands. This bold texture is the key to the exciting play of sweet, sour, and astringent sensations on the palate.

Prolong this eating pleasure by spreading this jam on English Muffins (see index) or tone it down with a muffin of contrasting texture such as Grapenuts Muffins or Banana Bran Muffins (see index).

2 pounds rhubarb stalks
12 ounces dried Calamata figs
1 cup water
2 cups sugar
1 tablespoon (or more to taste) fresh lemon juice

Rinse, trim, and cut rhubarb into ½-inch pieces. Cut off tough tips of fig stems and cut each fig into 8 bits.

Combine fruits and water in a deep, nonreactive 5-quart pan. Bring liquids to a simmer, cover, and cook slowly for 15 minutes. Lift the lid to stir regularly and adjust temperature so the mixture remains at a low simmer.

Add sugar ½ cup at a time and return to a boil for 5 minutes or until the jam is thick and holds its shape when cooled on a chilled plate. This is the plate test, illustrated on page 24.

Off heat, stir in the lemon juice. Cool another spoonful to taste it. Add more lemon juice if desired.

Fill hot, sterilized jars to within ⅛ inch of lips. Wipe the rims clean, attach new lids, and screw caps on tightly. Invert jars briefly for a quick vacuum seal or process in a boiling water bath, submerged by 1 inch, for 10 minutes.

YIELD: 6 cups

Green Tomato Jam

You may be surprised to find that unripe tomatoes cook into a mild, sweet jam. The lemon, apple, and cinnamon add greater subtlety.

Cornmeal Muffins and Buttermilk Currant Scones (see index) offer interesting taste and texture contrast.

2 pounds green tomatoes
2 lemons (8 ounces)
1 tart apple (4 ounces)
½ cup water
1 4-inch cinnamon stick
1 cup sugar

Remove the stem ends of the tomatoes and dice the tomatoes. (Chop them 2 at a time, quartered, in a food processor fitted with a steel blade, using rapid on-and-off motions.)

Remove the zest from the lemons with a zester (illustrated in Chapter 2). Cut off and discard the inner white peel. Halve the lemons and thinly slice, removing seeds.

Peel, quarter, core, and dice the apple.

Combine the tomatoes, lemon zest and slices, and apple pieces with the water and cinnamon stick in a heavy, nonreactive 4-quart pan.

Bring liquid to a boil, turn down the heat for a slow simmer, cover, and cook for 15 minutes. Lift the lid to check the simmer and stir every 5 minutes.

Uncover, turn up the heat to medium-high, and add the sugar ½ cup at a time. Cook, uncovered, for 10 minutes, stirring quite frequently. As the temperature rises to 210° F., the jam will thicken and begin to spit. Partly cover the pot to prevent spattering.

If the temperature has not reached 210° F. in 10 minutes, give the jam the cold plate test. Pour a teaspoon of jam on a cold plate and refrigerate it for 1 minute. Check the consistency of this cooled jam. If you want a thicker jam, cook it another 2-3 minutes and test again.

Off the heat, remove the cinnamon stick. Pour the jam into hot, sterilized jars to within ⅛ inch of lips. Wipe rims clean, attach new lids, and screw the caps on tightly. Invert the jars briefly for a quick vacuum seal or process for 10 minutes in a boiling water bath, submerged by 1 inch.

YIELD: 3½ cups

Spicy Cranberry Jam

Why should the cranberry be relegated to salad molds when it makes such a zesty preserve? This jam recipe is quite easy to prepare and a terrific topping with all holiday breads. Warm Butter Pecan Muffins or Whole Wheat English Muffins (see index) are my bread choices from this book.

You could easily freeze cranberry jam using my sorbet formula (see index) and serve it at the beginning or end of a rich winter meal as a festive and colorful palate freshener.

4 cups sugar
2 pounds cranberries
½ cup water
***Bouquet garni:* 1 4-inch cinnamon stick, ½ teaspoon fennel seed,**
    2 whole cloves, 3 allspice berries, 1 slice ginger

Warm 3½ cups sugar in a preheated 250° F. oven for 10 minutes.

Pick over and remove bruised cranberries before weighing them. Rinse them and combine with water and the remaining ½ cup sugar in a heavy, nonreactive 4-quart pot. Heat the berries and stir until liquids form and begin to boil. Maintain medium heat and stir frequently for 5 minutes.

Submerge *bouquet garni* in the cranberry mixture. Stir in the warm sugar ½ cup at a time, allowing the jam to return to the boil before adding more. Partly cover the pot if jam begins to spit. Continue to cook until the jam thickens and temperature rises to 214° F., no more than 20 minutes.

Off the heat, let the spices steep an additional 5 minutes before removing them. Pour the jam into hot, sterilized jars to within ⅛ inch of the lip. Wipe the rims clean, attach new lids, and screw the caps on tightly. Invert the jars for a quick vacuum seal or process in a boiling water bath, submerged by 1 inch, for 10 minutes.

YIELD: 6 cups

Plum Jam with Cardamom

Plum skins have a pleasant acidic tang that invites the heady fragrance of cardamom seeds.

This assertive jam tastes best with an equally vigorous bread like a Buckwheat Muffin or Whole Wheat English Muffin (see index).

2 pounds Italian plums
20 cardamom pods
⅓ cup water
1 cup sugar

Halve plums, remove pits, and finely chop. (If you are using a food processor, cut the plums with rapid on-and-off movements.) There will be about 3⅓ cups of plum pieces.

Tie cardamom pods in a piece of cheesecloth with cotton twine and crush them lightly with a rolling pin. Combine them with the plums, water, and sugar in a heavy, nonreactive 4-quart pan. Bring mixture to a boil, reduce to a steady simmer, and cook, uncovered, for 20 minutes or until the mixture is quite thick. Stir regularly to prevent sticking.

Off the heat, remove cardamom seeds. Fill hot, sterilized jars to within ⅛ inch of the lips. Wipe rims clean, attach new lids, and screw caps on tightly. Invert jars briefly for a quick vacuum seal or process in a boiling water bath, submerged by 1 inch, for 10 minutes.

YIELD: 3 cups

Damson Plum Jam

Since these petite plums, the color of eggplant, ripen quickly and are not widely grown, you may have to look hard to find them at the market. They are intensely sour when fresh, but their preserved essence of plum blossoms into a superb sweet-sour flavor.

This jam is crimson and spicy-sweet if cooked only to 114° F. As you continue to cook it to 118° F., it becomes darker, firmer, and tarter.

Pair this assertive jam with equally vigorous breads such as the Buckwheat Muffins or the Tea Brack (see index).

4 pounds Damson plums
1 cup water
Sugar

Rinse and stem plums. Place plums and the water in a heavy, nonreactive 5-quart pot and bring to a boil. Reduce heat to a gentle simmer, cover, and cook for 30 minutes. Lift the lid and stir every 5 minutes, crushing the plums against the side of the pot.

Let the cooked plums cool briefly, then pass them through a sieve or food mill to separate the pits and skins from the pulp. Measure the plum pulp and set aside ¾ cup sugar for every full cup of plums.

Combine plum pulp and 1 cup sugar in a deep 4- to 5-quart pan. Bring this to a boil. Begin adding sugar about ½ cup at a time, allowing the jam to return to the boil between additions. Hold back the last cup of sugar and simmer jam for 5 minutes.

Add ½ cup sugar and simmer another 5 minutes. Stir frequently to prevent sticking and partly cover the pot with a lid when it begins to spatter.

Pour in the last ½ cup sugar and stir well. A candy thermometer should be climbing into the 214-216° F. range. Off the heat, give jam the cold plate test. (Pour a teaspoon of hot jam onto a chilled plate and refrigerate it for 1 minute. The jam sample will cool to its finished consistency. If you like it soft, stop the cooking now.)

For a firmer jelled jam, cook the jam another 5 minutes for a total of up to 20 minutes and a temperature reading of up to 218° F. Stir almost constantly these last few minutes.

Off the heat, skim the jam and pour it into hot, sterilized jars to within ⅛ inch of the lips. Wipe off the rims, attach new lids, and screw caps on tightly. Invert the jars briefly for a quick vacuum seal or process in a boiling water bath, submerged by 1 inch, for 10 minutes.

YIELD: about 6 cups

Quince Jam

A ripe quince has such a rich apple perfume that you may hesitate to cook yours, preferring instead to cluster a few in a bowl to sit where their fragrance can be appreciated. Once you begin to prepare this fruit for cooking and see how hard and woody it is to cut, how positively astringent it is in the mouth, you will be convinced the market sold you the wrong fruit. Don't give up. Cooking and sweetening will thoroughly subdue and transform the quince into a soft and mild jam with a lovely apple scent.

Enjoy the delicacy of Quince Jam on Oatmeal Muffins or Drop Scones (see index).

1 quart water
1½ tablespoons fresh lemon juice
3 pounds quinces
1½ cups sugar

Combine water with 1 tablespoon of the lemon juice in a heavy, nonreactive 4-quart pan.

Peel, quarter, and core the quinces. Cut the quarters into eighths or smaller uniform pieces. As soon as each quince is cut, stir it into the acidulated water. This will keep them from discoloring.

Bring liquid to a boil, reduce the heat to a gentle simmer, cover, and cook the quinces for 30 minutes.

Remove about half of the tender quince pieces from the pot. Cut these into small pieces. Purée the pieces remaining in the pot with the liquid.

Return the quince pieces to the purée and return mixture to a simmer. Add the remaining ½ tablespoon of lemon juice and the sugar ½ cup at a time. The jam will be quite thick and will require frequent stirring to prevent sticking. Cook until the jam will hold its shape on a spoon, probably no more than 5 minutes.

Off the heat, ladle the jam into hot, sterilized jars to within ⅛ inch of the lips. Wipe rims clean, attach new lids, and screw caps on tightly. Invert the jars briefly for a quick vacuum seal or process for 10 minutes in a boiling water bath, submerged by 1 inch.

YIELD: 6 cups

Blueberry Jam with Mint

This recipe is a bit of a hybrid, mixing two steps from the preserve technique with the jam process. The sugar is added cup for cup with the fruit, and it is cooked to the jell point. However, the berries are never strained, steeped, or reduced but remain whole in the pot for the entire cooking process, which is typical of jam making. The result is a larger than usual yield of a sweet, delicate jam that is lightly jelled.

Try this jam with Butter Pecan Muffins or pour it over hot French Toast, Buckwheat Blinis, or the Giant Sunday Popover (see index).

2 pounds fresh or frozen dry-pack blueberries
½ cup water
Sugar
8 6-inch sprigs fresh mint

Combine berries with water in a heavy, nonreactive 5-quart pan. Turn heat to medium and cook, uncovered, until you can see liquid bubbling at the sides of the pan. Turn heat to medium-low, cover the pot, and cook berries another 20 minutes. Check to see that liquids are simmering.

Measure the berries and juices (there should be about 1 quart) and warm an equal volume of sugar in a 250° F. oven for 10 minutes.

Tie up 4 sprigs of mint with twine. Add them to the blueberries. Return the berries to the simmer and add sugar ½ cup at a time, trying to maintain the boil as much as possible.

Let jam boil and cook until it registers the jell temperature (boiling temperature as measured on your thermometer plus 8 degrees) in another 10-15 minutes. Off the heat, pull out the mint. Add the remaining 4 sprigs and crush them against the sides and bottom of the pan. Let them steep there for 5 minutes.

Remove the mint and fill hot, sterilized jars to within ⅛ inch of the lips. Wipe rims clean, attach new lids, and screw caps on tightly. Invert the hot jars momentarily for a quick seal or process in a boiling water bath, submerged by 1 inch, for 10 minutes.

YIELD: 5 cups

Boysenberry Jam

The Oregon boysenberries I used in this recipe were oblong and bristling with large juicy lobes. But, both fresh and cooked, they had a strangely ambivalent taste, favoring neither parent from which they were bred, the raspberry or blackberry. So I took the initiative and added a little raspberry brandy.

If you enjoy the taste and feel of firm berry bubbles, you will want to eat this jam on warm Buckwheat Muffins or Whole Wheat English Muffins (see index).

2 pounds boysenberries
1½ cups sugar
1½ tablespoons raspberry brandy

Combine boysenberries with ½ cup sugar in a heavy, nonreactive 4-quart pot. Heat and stir until liquid forms and begins to boil. Cook, uncovered, at an active simmer for 15 minutes, stirring regularly.

Stir in the remaining cup of sugar ½ cup at a time, allowing the mixture to return to the boil before adding more. Continue to cook the jam over medium-low heat for another 12-15 minutes, stirring frequently. The liquids will reduce, the jam will thicken, and the temperature will rise to 204° F.

Add the brandy and cook another minute.

Off the heat, pour jam into hot, sterilized jars to within ⅛ inch of the lips. Wipe the rims clean, attach new lids, and screw the caps on tightly. Invert the jars briefly for a quick vacuum seal or process them in a boiling water bath, submerged by 1 inch, for 10 minutes.

YIELD: 3 cups

Strawberry Rhubarb Jam

Although this classic combination is delicious on Risen Biscuits and English Muffins (see index), you can turn it into the main event in a number of desserts. Fill a prebaked tart shell with jam and decorate it with fresh strawberry halves and a red currant glaze. If the weather is too hot for baking, freeze it diluted with a simple syrup or light cream for a spectacular soft-frozen treat. The sensuous blend of silken rhubarb strands and soft, gritty berries is delicious at any temperature.

1 pound rhubarb (weighed before trimming)
2 pounds strawberries, washed, hulled, and halved
¼ cup water
10 strips lemon peel (approximately 3 inches long and ¼ inch
 wide)
2 cups sugar

Rinse, trim, and chop rhubarb into ½-inch pieces. Combine with strawberries, water, and lemon peel pieces in a heavy, nonreactive 4-quart pan.

Bring liquid to a boil and cook for 15 minutes, stirring regularly. (Fruit juices will concentrate and mixture will thicken noticeably.)

Add sugar ½ cup at a time, letting the liquids come to a simmer again before adding more. Continue to cook on medium heat for 10-15 minutes, stirring constantly, until the jam is thick and threatens to stick. Jam should reach a temperature of 210° F. Partially cover the pan should the liquids begin to spit during the last minutes of cooking.

Off the heat, skim and remove foam. Fill hot, sterilized jars to within ⅛ inch of lips. Wipe the rims clean, attach new lids, and screw caps on tightly. Invert jars quickly to vacuum seal or process in a boiling water bath, submerged by 1 inch, for 10 minutes.

YIELD: 4 cups

Blueberry Rhubarb Jam

Blueberry and rhubarb offer taste and aroma contrasts that cook into refreshing and quite pleasing preserves. They also leave a lovely tangled texture of silky strands and chewy bits in this jam. Grapenuts Muffins or Drop Scones (see index) would be my choices to serve with it.

1 pound fresh blueberries
1 pound rhubarb
¼ cup water
2½ cups sugar
½ tablespoon fresh lemon juice
Zest of 1 lemon

Rinse blueberries. Trim and rinse off rhubarb stalks. Cut them into ½-inch pieces.

Combine fruits in a heavy, nonreactive 4-quart saucepan with water and bring to a simmer. Cook the fruits over medium-low heat, uncovered, for 20 minutes, stirring regularly. (The mixture will be soft and thickened with large, ploppy bubbles.)

Begin adding sugar ½ cup at a time, returning the pot to a simmer before adding more. Pour in the lemon juice and the peel of 1 lemon removed with a zester (illustrated in Chapter 2). Continue to cook over medium heat, stirring frequently, for 15 minutes. Partially cover the pot to prevent splattering during the last few minutes of cooking. The temperature should reach 212° F.

Fill hot, sterilized jars to within ⅛ inch of the lips. Wipe the rims clean, attach new lids, and screw caps on tightly. Invert jars briefly for a quick seal or process in a boiling water bath, submerged by 1 inch, for 10 minutes.

YIELD: 4½ cups

Peach Pineapple Jam

Here is another jam in which one fruit with good acidity and an assertive texture—in this case, the pineapple—flatters the flavor and aroma of a sweet but retiring partner, the peach. This preserve offers the palate such an interesting texture and slightly tart finish that a bread with firm or contrasting texture would be welcome. Try one of the English Muffin recipes, Butter Pecan Muffins, or Tea Brack (see index).

1 ¼ pounds whole peaches
2 teaspoons fresh lemon juice
¾ pound peeled and cored fresh pineapple
1 ½ cups sugar

Dip the peaches in boiling water for 30 seconds and cool them under running water. Peel and halve them, removing the pits. Coarsely chop peaches and place them in a heavy, nonreactive 5-quart pan. Stir in the lemon juice to prevent discoloration.

Coarsely chop the pineapple before combining it with the peaches.

Bring fruits to a boil and simmer 8 minutes, stirring regularly.

When fruit mixture hisses as the spoon cleans the bottom of the pan, begin to add the sugar ½ cup at a time. Allow jam to return to the simmer before adding more. (Jam will start to spit as sugar is added, so protect yourself by covering the pot between sugar additions and by stirring regularly.) Cook another 5 minutes over medium heat or until the candy thermometer reads 210° F.

Fill hot, sterilized jars to within ⅛ inch of lips. Wipe the rims clean, attach dry lids, and screw the caps on tightly. Invert the jars briefly for a quick vacuum seal or process in a boiling water bath, submerged by 1 inch, for 10 minutes.

YIELD: 4 cups

Nectarine Orange Jam

High acidity in both nectarines and oranges makes this a zesty preserve. The cooling effects of fresh mint are especially pleasing here, if you have some in your garden. Grapenuts Muffins and Cream Scones (see index) taste wonderful with it.

4 pounds nectarines (7-8 cups peeled, pitted, and sliced)
4 large navel oranges (1½-2 pounds)
½ cup water
2 cups sugar
2 8-inch sprigs fresh mint (optional)

Dip the nectarines in simmering water for 30 seconds to loosen their skins. Peel and halve them to remove the pits. Thinly slice fruit pieces and place them in a heavy, nonreactive 4-quart pan.

Remove the zest from 2 oranges with a zester (illustrated in Chapter 2), and add it to the pan. Cut the peels from all the oranges and discard them. Halve the oranges and thinly slice them, removing seeds.

Combine oranges with nectarines, pour in the water, and bring to a simmer.

Cook, uncovered, stirring regularly, for 25 minutes. Stir more frequently as the liquids reduce. Lower heat if necessary to prevent fruit from sticking to the bottom of the pan. (The mixture will reduce to 6 cups.)

Begin adding sugar ½ cup at a time, trying to return the mixture to the boil quickly between additions. Continue cooking until the jam thickens and heats to 212° F., in 10-12 minutes. Partially cover the pot when it becomes thick and begins to spit. Remove the pan from the heat every 2 minutes to stir and loosen any pieces of fruit sticking to the pan bottom.

Off heat, put the mint sprigs in the jam, crushing them with a spatula or pestle against the side of the pan. Let them steep there for 5 minutes.

Remove the mint and fill hot, sterilized jars to within ⅛ inch of the lips. Wipe the rims clean, attach new lids, and screw caps on tightly. Invert momentarily for a quick seal or process in a boiling water bath for 10 minutes, submerged by 1 inch.

YIELD: 5 cups

Ginger Peach Jam

Fresh ginger root creates just the right exotic perfume and hot sensation on the tongue to provide a memorable accent for sweet peaches. After all, we say, "It's ginger peachy" only when everything is just right.

This is a jam to savor with English Muffins or Cornmeal Muffins (see index).

- **3 pounds peaches (6 medium)**
- **3 slices fresh ginger (size of a quarter)**
- **2 cups sugar**
- **1 tablespoon fresh lemon juice**
- **⅓ cup crystallized ginger (1½ ounces)**

Dip the peaches in simmering water for 30 seconds. Cool them under running water. Peel, halve, and remove pits. Cut each peach half in half and finely chop it. (If you are using a food processor, cut half the peach pieces at a time, making rapid on-and-off motions.)

Combine peaches with 1 cup sugar and ginger slices and bring to a boil in a deep, nonreactive 5-quart saucepan or stock pot. Add remaining cup of sugar ½ cup at a time along with the lemon juice.

Gently simmer the jam, stirring frequently. Take pot off the heat when stirring to avoid being spattered with hot jam. Cook for 30 minutes or until the liquid thickens and clears. Temperature will rise to 212° F., and volume should reduce to just under 4 cups.

Cut the crystallized ginger into pea-sized pieces. After skimming foam off the jam and removing the ginger slices, fold in crystallized ginger pieces.

Fill hot, sterilized jars to within ⅛ inch of the lips. Wipe rims clean, attach new lids, and screw caps on tightly. Quick-seal by inverting the jars briefly or process in a boiling water bath for 10 minutes, submerged by 1 inch.

YIELD: 4 cups

Serviceberry and Wild Black Raspberry Jam

The serviceberry tree is found among understory growth in temper-ate areas throughout the United States. Its slender, light gray branches and silver-green leaves most often take the shape of a spreading shrub that is quite distinctive. It nonetheless has other names, such as shad-bush, shadblow, and Juneberry. This last name refers to the small dark purple berries it produces in June and early July. Although their taste, fresh from the tree, is sweet and bland, these berries develop an enticing bouquet of roses when cooked. But for this trait you would never guess that the serviceberry is a member of the rose family.

Serviceberries have excellent pectin content and form an inspired partnership with wild, scratchy black raspberries that ripen at the same time in similar wooded settings.

Try this jam with English Muffins, Cream Scones, and Tea Brack (see index).

2 pounds serviceberries (3 cups simmered, strained juices)
¼ cup water
Pectin Stock, if needed (see index)
5 cups sugar
1 pound black raspberries (4 cups)
2 tablespoons fresh lemon juice

Combine the serviceberries with ¼ cup water and bring to a boil in a heavy, nonreactive 5-quart pot. Cook 15 minutes, stirring and crushing the berries to exude their juices. Strain this mixture for 4 hours or overnight. There will be about 3 cups strained juices. If there is more juice, reduce it to 3 cups. If there is less juice, add Pectin Stock (see index) to make 3 cups.

Measure the sugar onto a baking sheet or shallow tray. Warm it in a 250° F. oven for 10 minutes.

Bring the serviceberry juice to a simmer in a deep 5-quart pot. Stir in the black raspberries and cook slowly for 5 minutes.

(Recipe continues on following page.)

Pour in the lemon juice and warm sugar ½ cup at a time. Cook jam on medium-high heat, stirring regularly, until it reaches the jell temperature (the boiling temperature on your thermometer plus 8 degrees). This will take about 15 minutes.

Use a long-handled spoon for this recipe. Cover the pot when this jam begins to spatter as it nears 220° F. Check the temperature and stir off the heat every minute or so.

Fill hot, sterilized jars to within ⅛ inch of lips. Wipe rims clean, attach new lids, and screw caps on tightly. Either invert each jar quickly for a quick seal or process in a boiling water bath, submerged by 1 inch, for 10 minutes.

YIELD: 6 cups

4

NO-SUGAR JAMS

If jams can be taste-pleasing with as little as ¼ cup of sugar per pound of fruit, is it possible to create recipes with no added sugar at all? Yes, definitely. The availability of dried fruits, natural fruit juice concentrates, and canned fruits in unsweetened juices makes sugar-free preserving quite easy. All of these products have natural fruit sugar (fructose) and no refined sugar (sucrose).

These ingredients may be combined with fresh produce or used together to make thick, intensely flavorful jams. In the No-Sugar Peach Pineapple Jam with Apricots (see index) all three fruits are canned or dried. More often, the recipes combine fresh fruit with a juice concentrate and a spice, as in No-Sugar Orange Pineapple Jam (see index). In No-Sugar Pear and Blueberry Jam (see index), the fresh pears and blueberries are sweetened with only ½ cup of apple juice concentrate.

The easy and delicious possibilities of sugarless preserving will come as good news to nutrition-conscious cooks, calorie-counters, and those whose sugar intake must be limited for health reasons. No-sugar jams satisfy a craving for sweets in a totally natural way.

The reduced nature of dried fruit and juice concentrates makes no-sugar preserving a quick process. You can vary the texture of the fruits in these recipes a bit, but the consistency will always be thick enough to spread on breads and muffins. No-sugar jams will differ from their sweetened counterparts in two other significant ways: they have less sheen, and their rich fruit flavor leaves a slightly tart finish.

Such an assertive flavor profile makes sugarless jams good partners with sweet breads and muffins (see Chapter 8). Dilute them with equal volumes of cream or sugar syrup and freeze them to make exciting ice cream and sorbet flavors. You can also use them as interesting flavor accents in other fruit desserts (see Chapter 9).

These low-sugar jams do require careful processing. They are not as well protected from bacteria or molds as the preserves that jell or contain refined sugar. So seal in their freshness by submerging them by 1 inch in a boiling water bath for 10 minutes before storing. Keep them refrigerated after opening.

TECHNIQUE FOR MAKING NO-SUGAR JAMS

No-sugar jams begin with the combination of unsweetened juices with fruit pieces. In the No-Sugar Pineapple Raspberry Jam with Apricots, for example, pineapple juice joins the chopped apricots and half the raspberries in a deep pot. You cook the fruits in the juice, uncovered, until all the liquid has evaporated. The remaining half of the berries is added, then the pot is covered and the jam cooked but not stirred. The intent here is to stew the raspberries gently to draw out their juices (and prevent the fruit from sticking) while retaining their whole shape. You should shake the pan in this case to check for sticking. The jam is done when the berry juices have reduced and before the jam sticks. (See specific recipes for cooking times for both the first and second reductions.)

In recipes that call for whole spices these are added when the cooking begins and removed just before the jars are sealed.

Sugarless jams are packed in quilted jars and processed in a boiling water bath for 10 minutes, submerged by 1 inch of water (see directions in Chapter 2).

No-Sugar Peach Pineapple Jam with Apricots

This is a quick, easy recipe, especially if you have a food processor to do the cutting.

With such abundant flavor, a light buttery Drop Scone or Risen Biscuits (see index) would be the perfect complement.

1 1-pound can unsweetened peach pieces and juice
½ pound dried apricots, finely chopped
1 8-ounce can unsweetened, crushed pineapple in pineapple juice
1 tablespoon fresh lemon juice
1 4-inch stick cinnamon

Drain peaches and reserve the juices. Dice the peaches by hand or chop with rapid on-and-off motions in a food processor. Cut the apricots the same way. Combine peach pieces with their juice, apricots, crushed pineapple with its juice, and cinnamon stick in a heavy, nonreactive 4-quart saucepan.

Bring to a boil, reduce heat to a simmer, and stir constantly until the apricots are soft, almost all moisture is evaporated, and the jam is thickened. This will take about 10 minutes.

Off the heat, stir in lemon juice.

Fill hot, sterilized jars to within ⅛ inch of the lips. Wipe the rims clean, attach new lids, and screw the caps on tightly. Process jars in a boiling water bath, submerged by 1 inch, for 10 minutes.

YIELD: 3 cups

No-Sugar Pear and Blueberry Jam

*What could be simpler than a jam of pears and blueberries sim-
mered in apple juice? As cooking concentrates the juices, naturally sweet
flavors and fruit textures develop.*

*This preserve is a good stuffing for baked apples and is tasty on
Apple Cinnamon Muffins or Buttermilk Currant Scones (see index).*

1 pound blueberries
¼ cup water
1½ pounds Bartlett pears
½ cup unsweetened apple juice concentrate

Combine blueberries and water in a nonreactive 4-quart pan. Bring
water to a simmer, cover, and cook for 15 minutes. Lift the lid every 5
minutes to make sure the mixture is cooking slowly.

Peel, quarter, core, and dice the pears. Add them to the blueberries
with the apple juice. Raise the heat to medium under the pot and let the
pears cook and juices reduce over a 15-minute period.

Off the heat, spoon jam into hot, sterilized jars to within ⅛ inch of the
lips. Wipe the rims clean, attach new lids, and screw caps on tightly. Process
jams in a boiling water bath, submerged by l inch, for 10 minutes.

YIELD: 3½ cups

No-Sugar Peach Raspberry Jam

This classic combination works well without sugar when you use canned unsweetened peaches, which are less acidic than many fresh varieties. The raspberries, added after the peaches have been reduced, are cooked lightly so their shape and taste remain separate and clear.

Spread this preserve on Zucchini Bread or Butter Pecan Muffins (see index) for a real breakfast treat.

2 1-pound cans unsweetened peach halves in juice
8 ounces fresh red raspberries

Drain peaches and finely chop them by hand or with rapid on-and-off motions in a food processor, 1 pound at a time.

Combine peach pieces and juice in a heavy, nonreactive 3-quart saucepan. Bring to a boil, reduce heat to low, and simmer until almost all juice is evaporated from the peaches, stirring frequently. This will take up to 10 minutes. (When the mixture is ready, the bubbles will be small and close together. A spoon scraped across the bottom of the pan will make a hissing sound.)

Off the heat, add the raspberries, tossing them in the hot peaches. Cover the pan, return it to the low heat, and continue cooking another 5 minutes. Check the jam every minute or so. Shake the pan rather than stir it to redistribute the berries and juices.

Uncover the pan and turn up heat to medium. Stir gently, occasionally, until the jam is thickened again, not more than 5 minutes.

Fill hot, sterilized jars to within ⅛ inch of the lips. Wipe the rims clean, attach new lids, and screw the caps on tightly. Process in a boiling water bath, submerged by 1 inch, for 10 minutes.

YIELD: 3 cups

No-Sugar Apple Grape Jam

Apples and grapes are complementary fruits that hardly ever appear together. Without sugar, their flavors remain naturally tart, and the fresh, hot ginger root slices heighten these fruit tastes.

Serve Drop Scones and Butter Pecan Muffins (see index) with this jam.

3 pounds MacIntosh apples
1 12-ounce can unsweetened grape juice
1 cup water
2 slices ginger (size of a silver dollar)

Peel, core, quarter, and thinly slice apples.

Combine all ingredients in a heavy nonreactive 4-quart saucepan. Bring to a boil and simmer over low heat for 30 minutes or until the apples are soft and the juice is reduced enough to form a jamlike consistency.

Off the heat, remove ginger and fill hot, sterilized jars to within ⅛ inch of the lips. Tap jars on the counter to force out air pockets in the jam. Wipe the rims clean, attach new lids, and screw the caps on tightly. Process in a boiling water bath, submerge by 1 inch for 10 minutes.

YIELD: 3 cups

No-Sugar Apple Blackberry Jam

The choice of a tart, firm apple assures this jam a tangy finish and a texture of chunky fruit nuggets. For a sweeter flavor and softer texture, use MacIntosh or Jonathan apples.

You could serve this jam with Grapenuts Muffins or Tea Brack (see index).

3 Granny Smith or other firm, tart apples (1 ¼ pounds)
1 12-ounce can unsweetened apple juice concentrate
1 pound blackberries
2 4-inch sprigs of fresh bruised mint (optional)

Peel, quarter, and core the apples. Dice them coarsely and combine them in a 4-quart pan with the apple juice concentrate.

Bring the juice to a boil. Regulate the heat to maintain a slow simmer, cover, and cook the apples for 10 minutes.

Add the blackberries to the pot. Return the heat to a simmer, cover, and cook for 5 minutes.

Uncover the pot, turn the heat up to medium-high, and begin to actively reduce the liquids. Cook until a spoon drawn across the bottom of the pan causes a hissing sound. This will happen within 10 minutes.

Crush the mint stems and add them to the hot jam off the heat. Steep for five minutes or until their scent is noticeable. Remove mint and spoon the jam into hot, sterilized jars to within ⅛ inch of the lips. Wipe the rims clean, attach new lids, and screw caps on tightly. Process these jams in a boiling water bath, submerged by 1 inch, for 10 minutes.

YIELD: 3 cups

No-Sugar Cinnamon Nectarine Jam with Pineapple

Combined and reduced with pineapple juice, nectarines attain an intense sweet-sour balance. The cinnamon fragrance seems to sweeten this jam.

Butter Pecan Muffins, Cream Scones, and Risen Biscuits (see index) are all excellent with this jam. This flavor would also make a refreshing sorbet if you merely dilute it with simple syrup and freeze it on a sheet cake pan (see index for sorbet recipe).

3 pounds fresh nectarines, pitted and coarsely chopped
3 6-ounce cans frozen unsweetened pineapple juice concentrate
1 cinnamon stick

Combine nectarine pieces with juice concentrate and cinnamon in a heavy nonreactive 4-quart saucepan.

Bring liquid to a boil, reduce heat, and simmer over medium heat, stirring constantly, until mixture thickens and most moisture is evaporated. This will take 12-15 minutes.

Off the heat, remove cinnamon stick. Fill hot, sterilized jars to within ⅛ inch of the lips. Wipe the rims clean, attach new lids, and screw the caps on tightly. Process in a boiling water bath, submerged by 1 inch, for 10 minutes.

YIELD: 4½ cups

No-Sugar Pineapple Raspberry Jam with Apricots

An excellent way to savor the sweet-sour taste harmony and complex texture of this jam is on Cream Scones or Risen Biscuits (see index).

2 cups unsweetened pineapple juice
12 ounces fresh red raspberries
6 ounces dried apricots, finely chopped

Combine juice, half the raspberries, and all the apricot pieces in a deep, heavy nonreactive 4-quart saucepan.

Simmer over medium-low heat until almost all the liquid has evaporated, about 10 minutes.

Add remaining raspberries. Lower heat, cover the pan, and stew whole berries gently for 5 minutes. Gently shake the pan to determine moisture level, but do not stir. Mixture is ready when, again, almost all moisture is evaporated, in about 5 minutes.

Fill hot, sterilized jars to within ⅛ inch of the rim, taking care to keep the soft, whole raspberries intact. Wipe the rims clean, attach new lids, and screw the caps on tightly. Process in a boiling water bath, submerged by 1 inch, for 10 minutes.

YIELD: 3 cups

No-Sugar Blueberry Orange Jam

In this recipe whole blueberries retain their watery sweetness as a distinct, refreshing contrast to the acidic tang of the oranges.

This jam is delicious on Oatmeal Muffins and Zucchini Bread (see index).

3 navel oranges
1 12-ounce can unsweetened orange juice concentrate
1 pound fresh blueberries

Remove the zest from the oranges with a zester (illustrated in Chapter 2). Cut off and discard the inner white peel. Thinly slice the oranges.

Combine juice concentrate, zest, and orange slices in a nonreactive 4-quart saucepan. Bring to a boil and cook on medium-high until most of the liquid is evaporated, 5-10 minutes.

Off the heat, stir in the blueberries. Cover, reduce the heat to low, and simmer the jam 5 minutes.

Uncover the pot and raise the heat. Cook another minute or two, stirring continuously, until mixture thickens.

Fill hot, sterilized jars to within ⅛ inch of the lips. Wipe the rims clean, attach new lids, and screw the caps on tightly. Process in a boiling water bath, submerged by 1 inch, for 10 minutes.

YIELD: 3⅓ cups

No-Sugar Pear and Grape Jam

This variation of the Pear and Grape Preserves (see index) has a for-matable history. Pear and grape juice raisone, as it is called in France, has been made by farmers in Burgundy for several hundred years. A recipe for it first appeared in A. A. Parmentier's early nineteenth-century cookbook in response to a request by Napoleon I for the development of sugar-free foods. (France at that time was being cut off from its sugar supply by the English.)

3 pounds ripe Bartlett pears
1 12-ounce can unsweetened grape juice concentrate

Peel, quarter, and core the pears. Thinly slice the pears and combine with juice concentrate in a heavy, nonreactive 4-quart pan. Cook for 30 minutes, until thickened. Pour into jars, process in a boiling water bath, and store as in the recipe for Pear and Grape Preserves.

YIELD: 3 cups

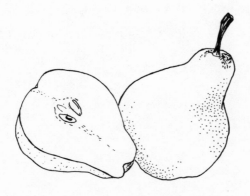

No-Sugar Orange Fig Jam

This jam blends intensely sweet dried figs with tart orange juice concentrate and barely cooked fresh orange sections.

Drop Scones fresh off the griddle or warm Butter Pecan Muffins (see index) taste wonderful with this jam.

8 large dried figs (6 ounces)
1 12-ounce can frozen unsweetened orange juice concentrate
3 navel oranges (1 ½ pounds)

Remove tough stem tips of figs and chop each fig into 10 pieces. Combine them in a heavy nonreactive 4-quart saucepan with the juice concentrate and bring to a boil. Cook at a simmer until the mixture thickens, in 5-10 minutes. Stir steadily after the first 3 minutes. When jam is thick enough, rising bubbles will lift the surface with plopping sounds. Remove pan from the heat.

Slice the peel from the oranges with a knife and discard it. Cut down between the membrane and the pulp to release each segment, discarding membranes. Stir orange pieces into hot jam. Simmer for another 5 minutes until the jam thickens again.

Fill hot, sterilized jars to within ⅛ inch of the lips. Wipe the rims clean, attach new lids, and screw the caps on tightly. Process jars in a boiling water bath, submerged by 1 inch, for 10 minutes.

YIELD: 2½ cups

No-Sugar
Orange Pineapple Jam

Cloves and allspice berries are flattering spices for this jam, but you could experiment with others.

Banana Bran Muffins and Oatmeal Muffins (see index) are good complements to this preserve. It is also very refreshing when diluted with simple syrup and frozen as a sorbet (see index for sorbet recipe).

3 pounds navel oranges (4 cups peeled and coarsely chopped)
1 12-ounce can frozen pineapple orange juice concentrate
2 cups crushed pineapple, after draining
3 whole cloves
4 whole allspice berries

Combine all fruit ingredients in a heavy, nonreactive 5-quart saucepan. Tie spices in a piece of cheesecloth with cotton twine and stir them into the pot. Bring mixture to a boil over high heat. Reduce heat to medium-high and cook until thickened, stirring frequently, as long as 20 minutes.

Off the heat, remove spices and fill hot, sterilized jars to within ⅛ inch of the lips. Wipe the rims clean, attach new lids, and screw the caps on tightly. Process jars in a boiling water bath, submerged by 1 inch, for 10 minutes.

YIELD: 3 cups

5
JELLIES

Want to know the secret of making perfect jelly every time? One that has a firm, supple texture when you spoon it from a jar? A jelly that melts easily in the mouth, exuding sweet-sour sensations and the fresh scent of fruit? The recipes in this chapter are based on a practical formula arrived at after much experimentation. They should work as well for you as they have for me.

First, the jellies are made from fruits and berries which nature blessed with high pectin content: grapes, apples, black raspberries, cranberries, and currants. The flavor potential of these fruits is brought out through the addition of only as much sugar as is needed for a jell.

The strict routine of jelly making leaves little room for changes in procedure. All the jellies are cooked, strained, reduced, and sweetened alike, using the same proportions, pectin level, and jelling temperature. Nevertheless, there are new taste sensations to try. If you have grown up thinking grape jelly is for peanut butter sandwiches, you may be delightfully surprised by my thyme-scented version (see index). Similarly, the cardamom in Red Currant Jelly (see index) mellows the berries' tartness in a most exciting way.

The range of jelly flavors can be greatly expanded by simply using Apple Pectin Stock as the medium. You can introduce herbs, spices, or bits of tasty peppers and transform a jelly into a condiment. Pectin stock will also jell well if diluted with highly reduced wines and liqueurs. With the formula for Wine Jelly, you can create flavors using your own favorite grape and aperitif wines.

JELLY-MAKING TECHNIQUES

Since there are two cooking periods in jelly making, it is best to start early in the day or spread your work over two days. The first major task involves cooking the fruits and then straining them to separate pulp from juice. In the second cooking period the juice is brought to the jell.

Preparing the Fruit

1. First, rinse, drain, and place the fruit in a large, nonreactive pot. Coarsely chop larger fruits. Remove stems, leaves, and stalks, but include cores, pits, or seeds.

2. Each recipe specifies whether to bake the fruit or cook it on top of the stove. Cooking the fruit for 20-45 minutes guarantees that all the juices are exuded and the fruits or berries are collapsed. In some recipes the fruit pieces are stirred and crushed against the side of the pot to hasten this process.

3. The cooked fruits are then strained to separate the juices from the pulp. Use a sieve or colander or purchase a jelly bag designed for straining. Line all metal strainers with dampened, fine-mesh cheesecloth. Juices from 3 pounds of berries or grapes strain in an hour or two. Four pounds of fruit take up to three hours.

Experiments comparing the results of overnight straining with those of three-hour straining have shown that the longer period rarely yields more than an additional ½ cup of juice. Sometimes the longer period yields juice higher in pectin level than the juice strained in 3 hours; other times it does not. You might want to strain pulpy apples overnight, but otherwise, the three-hour period will usually suffice. As you acquire experience, your own judgment will dictate the best straining time.

There is no way, incidentally, to hurry this straining process. Putting pressure on the sieve will only force out fine bits of fruit and destroy the clarity of your jelly.

Cooking the Jelly

1. All the strained juices in these recipes are cooked a second time with an equal volume of sugar. The only exceptions to this rule are grapes and apples which are reduced somewhat before sugar is added, to concentrate their pectin. (The exception to this exception is the greening apple juice, which is treated as the majority of the fruit juices are.)

When the quantity of sugar required is greater than 3 cups, it should be warmed for 10 minutes in a 250° F. oven. Warm sugar will dissolve in the boiling liquid more quickly than if it were at room temperature.

2. Add the required amount of sugar ½ cup at a time, allowing the juices to return to the boil before adding more. When all the sugar has been added, the jelly will return to a boil that cannot be stirred down. This is the time for you to adjust the heat so the liquid remains at a steady boil and to get ready to check for the jell. Each recipe indicates about how long it will take to reach the jell after all the sugar is added.

A candy thermometer (illustrated in Chapter 3) is the most accurate tool for measuring the jell point. Check it in boiling water before you use it in jelly. The jell point (or temperature) is 8 degrees above the boiling temperature measured on your thermometer. As you know from Chapter 2, on technique, the spoon test will verify when the temperature has reached 216° F. You can also double-check the jell temperature with the cold-plate test described in Chapter 2.

Each recipe calls for boiling the jelly for a full minute after it reaches the jell point. This is yet another way to assure a complete jell.

3. After the jelly comes off the range, it may need to be skimmed of foam before being poured into jars. It can also wait 3-5 minutes while you pull the sterilized jelly jars from their boiling water bath.

4. Pour the jelly with a ladle through a funnel into the hot, clean jelly glasses. Fill them to within ½ inch of the rims. Cover the jars lightly with plastic wrap to protect them from organisms in the air and wait for the top surface to set. This may take only 15 minutes or as long as an hour.

5. Sugar in the jell ties up the water so well that only a thin (⅛-inch) layer of paraffin is needed to seal the surface of the jelly from the air. Melt this wax in the pitcher you have made for it from a shortening can (see Chapter 2) by placing the can in a saucepan filled with two inches of water. Let the water come to a boil, then take it off the heat; the water will keep the wax melted for 15 minutes.

6. Wipe the inner rims of the jelly jars clean so the wax will make good contact with the glass. Pour ⅛ inch melted paraffin over the surface of the jelly, tilting and turning the jar to seal the edges and evenly distribute the wax before it hardens. If you see any air bubbles or cracks in the paraffin after it dries, pour on another thin coating following the same procedure.

A jelly that passes all the tests for a jell but refuses to set should be allowed to cool to room temperature. Occasionally jellies can take longer than an hour to jell. Should your jelly not jell, review the remedies in Chapter 2 under "Why the Jelly Won't Jell." If it does not make it as a jelly, use this new fruit syrup to make ice cream toppings or a sauce for fresh fruit.

Master Recipe for Grape Jelly

Homemade grape jelly puts the store-bought versions to shame. It jells easily and has an expansive sweet-sour flavor. Banana Bran Muffins and Cream Scones (see index) make delicious partners for it.

4 pounds Concord grapes
½ cup water
4 cups sugar

Rinse and remove the grapes from their stems. Combine grapes with water in a heavy, nonreactive 4-quart pot. Bring to a boil, slow to a simmer, cover the pot, and cook for 30 minutes. Occasionally stir and crush the grapes against the side of the pan.

Strain juices from the fruit through cheesecloth for 3 hours or overnight. Measure and reduce juices to 4 cups. Warm 4 cups of sugar in a 250° F. oven for 10 minutes.

Bring grape juice to a boil. Add sugar ½ cup at a time, allowing liquid to return to the boil before adding more. Cook to the jell point, which is 8 degrees above the boiling point measured on your thermometer. This will take about 5 minutes. Maintain the boil for a full minute after reaching the jell.

Off the heat, skim and ladle into hot, sterilized jelly jars to within ½ inch of the lip. Cover jars loosely with plastic wrap until the top sets. Melt the paraffin over water. Wipe the inner mouth of the jars clean. Pour on ⅛ inch wax, rotating the jars at an angle to seal the edges and make an even coating.

Let jelly cool to room temperature overnight. Cover with snap-on lids and store in a cool, dry place.

YIELD: 4½ cups

Grape Jelly Variations

Grape Jelly with Fresh Thyme

Steep completed jelly in the pan with 3 6-inch sprigs of fresh thyme. Remove them and proceed to fill and seal the jars.

Spicy Grape Jelly

Tie one 4-inch cinnamon stick, 4 allspice berries, 4 whole cloves, and 3 cardamom pods in cheesecloth with cotton twine. Cook the spices with the grape juice as the sugar is added. Remove before filling jars.

Crabapple Jelly

The flavor of crabapples can vary quite a bit from one tree to the next, a fact that makes the quality of your jelly hard to predict unless you use fruit from the same tree year after year. Even then, some harvests are better than others. In fact, one attraction of preserving as an annual ritual is its ability to capture the subtle pulse of nature.

It's a pleasure to spread this jelly on a hot Butter Pecan Muffin (see index) and watch it begin to warm and soften just as you eat it.

5 pounds crabapples
Enough water to cover crabapples (approximately 2 quarts)
Sugar

Stem and halve the apples. Combine them with water in a heavy, nonreactive 8-quart pot. The water should almost cover the apples.

Bring water to a boil, reduce to a simmer, and cook, partially covered, for 45 minutes.

Strain the apples through cheesecloth for 3 hours or overnight.

Measure the apple juices and warm an equal volume of sugar for 10 minutes in a 250° F. oven.

Bring the juices to a boil and stir in the sugar ½ cup at a time, waiting for the mixture to return to the boil before adding more. Cook over medium-high heat until it reaches the jell temperature, which is 8 degrees higher than the boiling point measured on your thermometer. This may take as long as 15 minutes.

Maintain the boil for a full minute after reaching the jell.

Off the heat, skim the jelly and ladle it into hot, sterilized jelly jars to within ½ inch of the lip. Cover the jars loosely with plastic wrap until the tops are set. Melt the paraffin in its pitcher over hot water. Wipe clean the inner rims of the jars. Pour a layer of hot wax ⅛ inch thick over each jelly surface, tilting and rotating the jar to seal the edges and cover the top evenly.

Allow the jelly to cool to room temperature, preferably overnight, before attaching snap-on lids, labeling and storing.

YIELD: 9 cups

Cinnamon Cranberry Apple Jelly

Picture this ruby-bright jelly as a beautiful holiday offering with a stick of cinnamon tied in green ribbon on its cap. It would taste delicious spread on any rich brioche *breads or Christmas* stollen. *Tea Brack or Butter Pecan Muffins (see index) would be my serving choices from the breads in this book.*

2 pounds cranberries
2 pounds Granny Smith or Jonathan apples
6 cups water
Sugar
1 stick cinnamon

Rinse and pick over the cranberries before weighing them. Coarsely chop the apples, removing stems only. Combine fruits in a heavy, nonreactive 5-quart pan. Pour the water over them and bring to a boil. Reduce heat to a simmer, partially cover, and cook for 20 minutes.

Strain the juice through a cheesecloth-lined sieve for 3 hours or overnight. Measure the juices and pour an equal volume of sugar onto a shallow baking sheet.

Preheat the oven to 250° F. and warm the sugar for 10 minutes.

Add the cinnamon stick to the cranberry-apple juice and bring to a boil in a 5-quart nonreactive pot. Stir in the warm sugar ½ cup at a time, returning the liquid to a boil before adding more. Let the jelly boil until it reaches the jell point, which is 8 degrees above the boiling temperature measured on your thermometer. This will take about 5 minutes. Maintain the boil for a full minute after reaching the jell point.

Off the heat, skim foam from the surface and pour jelly into hot, sterilized jelly jars to within ½ inch of the lips. Cover the jars loosely with plastic wrap until the top sets.

Melt the paraffin in its pitcher over water. Wipe clean the inner rims of the jars. Pour on a layer of wax ⅛ inch thick. Tilt and rotate the jars to seal the edges and make an even coating. Let the jelly come to room temperature overnight before attaching snap-on lids and storing.

YIELD: 7 cups

Aromatic Herb Jelly

The warm perfume of fresh herbs in scented jelly will flood your senses with memories of a summer garden. Herb fragrances are evocative but fragile, so I spread this jelly on simple, buttery Cream Scones or Risen Biscuits (see index).

**3 pounds Granny Smith or Jonathan apples, stemmed and
coarsely chopped**
1 quart water
2 4-inch sprigs fresh herb leaves (see Note)
4 cups sugar, warmed

Combine apples and water in a heavy, nonreactive 5-quart pot. Bring water to a boil, reduce heat to a simmer, and cook, covered, for 40 minutes.

Strain the apple juices through a fine cheesecloth-lined sieve. Let the apples drain for 3 hours or overnight.

Measure the apple juice. Bring to a boil and reduce to 4 cups. Skim off the foam at the end of this step.

While the juice is reducing, preheat the oven to 250° F. Measure the sugar onto a shallow baking sheet and warm it for 10 minutes in the oven. Rinse and pat dry the herb leaves.

Stir the herb sprigs into the hot apple juice and crush them against the bottom and sides of the pot. Bring the juice to a boil and begin to add the warm sugar, ½ cup at a time, allowing it to return to the boil before adding more.

After all the sugar is added, continue to simmer and test the temperature with a candy thermometer or an instant thermometer until it reaches the jell temperature, which is 8 degrees above the boiling temperature measured on your thermometer. This will take 5-7 minutes.

Off the heat, skim off herb sprigs and scum. Ladle the jelly through a funnel into hot, sterilized jars. Cover them lightly with plastic wrap. When the tops have set, in about 20 minutes, add 1 perfect herb leaf to each jar.

While the jelly is cooling, melt the paraffin in its pitcher over water. Wipe clean the inner rims of the jars and pour on a ⅛-inch-thick layer of wax. Rotate the jars at a slight angle to seal the edges and evenly coat the top.

Let the jars come to room temperature before adding snap-on lids, labeling, and storing in a cool, dark, dry place.

Note: Herbs such as basil, sweet woodruff, lemon thyme, rosemary, sage, and the many mint varieties make fragrant additions to jelly. A more experimental cook could try bay leaf, lavender, or coriander leaves. The oils in lemon verbena and marjoram are excellent but rather fragile. You will add double the amount of these herbs to steep in the jelly.

YIELD: 5 to 6 cups

Black Raspberry Jelly

This luxurious jelly will flatter any bread or biscuit, particularly a chewy English Muffin (see index).

6 pounds black raspberries (8-9 pints)
Sugar
2 tablespoons fresh lemon juice

Preheat the oven to 350° F. Pick over the berries and divide them between 2 heavy, nonreactive 4-quart pots. Cover and bake berries for 45 minutes. If both pots will not fit in the oven, cook one on the stovetop for 15 minutes, covered, then cook another 5 minutes uncovered. Stir and crush the berries against the side of the pan. Remove the pots from the oven and cook them another minute or two on the range, stirring and crushing berries. Strain the berries through cheesecloth for 3 hours.

Measure the berry juice and warm an equal volume of sugar in a 250° F. oven for 10 minutes. Bring the juices to a boil in a heavy, nonreactive 5-quart pan. Add the sugar ½ cup at a time, allowing the liquid to return to the boil before adding more. Stir in the lemon juice after the first cup of sugar has been added. Let the liquid boil until it reaches the jell temperature, which is 8 degrees above the boiling temperature measured on your thermometer. This will take about 10 minutes. Maintain the boil for a full minute after reaching the jell.

Off the heat, skim jelly and ladle into hot, sterilized jelly jars to within ½ inch of the lids. Cover loosely with plastic wrap until the top sets. Melt the paraffin in its pitcher over water. Wipe clean the inner mouth of the jars. Pour on a ⅛-inch-thick layer of wax. Rotate the jars to distribute evenly and seal the edges. Let the jars cool overnight to room temperature.

Cover with snap-on lids and store in a cool, dry place.

YIELD: almost 4 cups

Master Recipe for Red Currant Jelly

This is the quintessential jelly, with its exquisitely tart flavor, bright ruby color, and shimmering jell. It flatters rich breads and muffins as a preserve and makes a great poaching medium and sauce for peaches, pears, and apples. My favorite bread partners for this vigorous jelly are Buckwheat Muffins and Whole Wheat English Muffins (see index).

4 pounds red currants
Sugar

Preheat the oven to 350° F. Rinse currants but leave berries on their stems. Place in a heavy, nonreactive 5-quart pot and bake, covered, for 40 minutes. Strain 3 hours or overnight.

Measure the currant juice and warm an equal volume of sugar in a 250° F. oven for 10 minutes. Place juice in a 4-quart saucepan and bring to a boil. Stir in the sugar ½ cup at a time. Bring liquid to jell temperature, which is 8 degrees above the boiling temperature measured on your thermometer. This will take up to 10 minutes. Maintain the boil for a full minute after reaching the jell.

Off the heat, skim off foam. Pour jelly into hot, sterilized jelly glasses to within ½ inch of the lips. Cover with plastic wrap until tops have set. Wipe clean the inner rims of the jars. Melt paraffin and pour on a ⅛-inch-thick layer, rotating each glass at an angle to seal the edges and form an even layer. Prick any bubbles that appear in the jelly or wax.

Let the jars cool to room temperature. Cover with snap-on lids and store in a cool, dry spot.

YIELD: 5¼ cups

Red Currant Jelly with Cardamom

Bouquet garni: 1 2-inch stick cinnamon, 10 bruised cardamom seeds

Add the spices tied in a cheesecloth to the strained currant juices. Proceed with the master recipe. Remove spices just before completed jelly is poured into jars.

Apple Pectin Stock

With a supply of this apple juice concentrate, you can make virtually any jelly flavor you desire. The pectin in the apple will contribute generously to a jell; its subtle fragrance will defer to the scents of fruits, herbs, and spices.

This recipe will give you enough stock for two recipes of Wine Jelly or as many as four recipes in which lesser amounts are needed. To avoid being caught short, make more than one recipe of stock when time allows and store it in your larder, either vacuum-sealed or frozen. Fresh stock will refrigerate well for up to two weeks.

4 pounds Granny Smith or Jonathan apples
6 cups water

Stem the apples and coarsely chop them, including seeds, skins, and cores. Place pieces in a heavy, nonreactive 5-quart pot. Pour in 6 cups water. Bring pot to a boil, reduce heat to a simmer, and cook, partly covered, for 45 minutes.

Strain apples through damp cheesecloth for 3 hours or overnight. There will be 6-7 cups of apple juice.

Reduce juice to 3 cups.

If you are going to be using the stock within the next 2 weeks, simply pour it into a clean storage jar and refrigerate. Stock can also be frozen in clean plastic containers.

To vacuum-seal the stock, fill hot, sterilized jars to within ⅛ inch of the lips. Wipe the rims clean, attach new lids, and screw on the caps. Invert the jars briefly for a quick vacuum seal or process in a boiling water bath, submerged by 1 inch, for 10 minutes.

YIELD: 3 cups

(A variation of this recipe follows.)

Pectin Stock Using Greening Apples

4 pounds greening apples
2 quarts water

Follow the directions for Apple Pectin Stock above, but cook the apples and water for only 20 minutes. You want them to exude their juices but not to cook into applesauce.

This apple variety will strain out to about 1 cup juice per pound of apples. There is no need to reduce this stock.

YIELD: 4 cups

Wine Jelly

Jellies made from good-quality varietal wines with a fruity scent and good acid, such as Cabernet Sauvignon and Chardonnay, are particularly flavorful. Since the jelling action is provided by the pectin stock alone, you are free to experiment with this preserve formula. For example, why not reduce a red wine with a bouquet of your favorite spices for a mulled wine jelly?

Tea Brack, Zucchini Bread, and Cream Scones (see index) pair well with this tart jelly.

1 bottle wine (3⅓ cups)
3 cups sugar
1½ cups Apple Pectin Stock (see index)

Reduce the wine to 1½ cups in a heavy, nonreactive 4-quart pot.
Warm the sugar for 10 minutes in a 250°F. oven.
Combine pectin stock with wine and bring to a simmer. Add the sugar ½ cup at a time, allowing liquid to return to the boil before adding more. Continue to boil until it reaches the jell temperature, that is, 8 degrees above boiling temperature measured on your thermometer. This will take 10–15 minutes.
Skim the jelly and ladle it into hot, sterilized jelly jars. Cover the jellies loosely with plastic wrap until the top has set.

Melt the paraffin in its pitcher over water. Wipe the inner rims of the jars clean and pour on a ⅛-inch-thick layer of wax. Rotate the jar at a slight angle to seal the edges and evenly coat the surface.

Let jars come to room temperature before adding snap-on lids, labeling, and storing.

YIELD: 3 cups

Kir Cocktail Jelly

If you want to transform your favorite wine aperitif into a jelly, plan to experiment with small batches until you get the right flavor balance. This particular combination of white wine and crème de cassis has a delicate taste of grape and the aroma of black currants. It is delicious with a Cream Scone or Grapenuts Muffin (see index).

1 bottle Chablis (3¼ cups)
3 tablespoons crème de cassis (Dijon brand)
1½ cups Apple Pectin Stock (see index)
3 cups sugar

Reduce wine over high heat to 1 cup in a nonreactive pot. Stir in the cassis and stock.

Bring liquid to a boil in a nonreactive 5-quart pot and add the sugar ½ cup at a time, returning it to a boil before adding more. Continue to cook at a boil until liquid reaches the jelling temperature, that is, 8 degrees above the boiling temperature measured on your thermometer. This will take about 10 minutes.

Off the heat, skim and ladle jelly into hot, sterilized jelly jars. Cover jelly jars with plastic wrap until the top has set.

Melt the paraffin in its pitcher over water. Wipe the inner rims of the jars clean and pour on a ⅛-inch-thick layer of wax. Rotate the jar at a slight angle to seal the edges and evenly coat the surface. Let the jars come to room temperature before adding snap-on lids, labeling, and storing in a dark, cool, dry spot.

YIELD: 2¾ cups

Sweet Pepper Jelly

The sweet, woody fragrance of red peppers blends well with apple stock in this recipe. It also makes a beautiful jelly, full of swimming bits of bright pepper gems. This is a delicious jelly to take along on a late summer picnic with Cornmeal Muffins, Risen Biscuits, or Whole Wheat English Muffins (see index).

1 each red and green sweet peppers (8 ounces total)
3 cups Apple Pectin Stock (see index)
Sugar
Zest of 1 lemon

Cut the peppers in half to remove stems, interior seeds, and membranes. Mince the flesh and add it to the pectin stock in a heavy, nonreactive 4-quart pot. Bring this to a boil, reduce heat to a simmer, and cook for 10 minutes.

Skim the liquid, measure it, and set aside an equal volume of sugar. Return the pepper mixture to a simmer and begin adding the sugar ½ cup at a time, allowing the liquid to return to the boil before adding more.

After all the sugar is added, let the jelly boil until it reaches the jell point, which is 8 degrees above the boiling temperature measured on your thermometer. This will take about 5 minutes. Maintain the boil for a full minute after reaching the jell.

Skim the jelly and stir in the lemon zest that has been removed with a zester (illustrated in Chapter 2). Ladle it into hot, sterilized jelly jars to within ½ inch of the lips. Cover jellies loosely with plastic wrap until the pepper pieces stay suspended when stirred down. This will take from 20 minutes to an hour.

Melt the paraffin in its pitcher over water and pour on a ⅛-inch-thick layer to cover the jelly. Wipe clean the inner rims of the jars. Rotate the jar at an angle to seal the edges and make an even coating. Let jars come to room temperature before adding snap-on lids, labeling, and storing.

YIELD: 3¾ cups

Jalapeño Pepper Jelly

A little hot pepper goes a long way in fragrant apple stock. To tame this searing hot jelly, spread it on cooled Cornmeal Muffins or Buckwheat Muffins (see index). If there is cream cheese to slather on in place of butter, so much the better.

2 jalapeño peppers
3 cups Apple Pectin Stock (see index)
Sugar
½ tablespoon fresh lemon juice

Wear rubber gloves and work on a nonporous surface to stem, halve, seed, and mince the jalapeño peppers.

Combine them with the stock in a heavy, nonreactive 4-quart pan. Bring liquid to a boil, reduce to a simmer, and cook for 10 minutes.

Off the heat, skim and measure. Set aside an equal volume of sugar.

Return the pepper mixture to the boil and add sugar ½ cup at a time, letting it return to the boil before pouring in more. Stir in the lemon juice and let the mixture boil until it reaches the jell point, which is 8 degrees above the boiling point measured on your thermometer. This will take about 5 minutes. Maintain the boil for a full minute after reaching the jell.

Skim the jelly and ladle it into hot, sterilized jelly jars to within ½ inch of the lips. Cover them loosely with plastic wrap and wait until the pepper pieces stay suspended when stirred down, from 15 minutes to 1 hour.

Wipe clean the inner rims of the jars. Melt paraffin in its pitcher and pour a sheet ⅛ inch thick on the jelly. Rotate the jars to seal the edges and make an even coating. Cool them to room temperature before putting on the snap-on lids, labeling, and storing.

YIELD: 3 cups

Three-Alarm Jalapeño Pepper Jelly

Mince 4 jalapeño peppers and proceed with the master recipe above.

6

MARMALADES

The history of marmalade is full of international lore. The first English recipe appeared in a cookbook published in 1524. Its source, the Portuguese *marmelado* preserve, was popular in England at the time.

The original marmalade took its name from the *marmelo* quince. This is a hard and astringent fruit when fresh, but it cooks down to a surprisingly soft, sweet preserve with an intense apple perfume. Today's bittersweet marmalades, shimmering jellies with suspended bits of citrus pulp and peel, could not be more different. The change dates from a time long ago, when English marmalade became identified with the fiercely bitter Seville orange. One story credits the Scotsman James Keiller and his wife with making the first orange marmalade, in the 18th century. But Keiller did not create the preserve, though his recipe helped to popularize it. English recipes for bitter orange marmalade were commonplace as early as the 17th century.

Another unlikely but curious theory links the word *marmalade* with the French expression *"Marie malade."* Could the sick Marie referred to here be Mary, Queen of Scots? Restorative marmalades were indeed popular during her 16th-century reign. These preserves included oranges and herbal ingredients of great medicinal importance. Could the beneficial effect of its vitamin C content have been recognized before it was scientifically proven? Unfortunately, the later history of preserving fails to affirm any connection, since many noncitrus fruit preserves have been called *marmalades* since the 18th century.

Perhaps it was the exhilarating interplay of sweet, sour, and bitter tastes that caused medieval herbalists to use early orange marmalades as medical therapy. It's this special taste complexity that I enjoy most in them. And all my marmalades, you will find, use some degree of bitter peel to amplify fruit flavors.

There are two other important reasons for including the bitter peel of a citrus fruit in preserves. For one, the white inner peel and pips (seeds) are the main source of pectin in citrus fruit. They are the natural jelling agent, unless a high-pectin fruit such as apple or cranberry is also present. In addition, the outer rind of citrus fruits contains perfumed floral oils that characterize the scent of each fruit.

Think about how this sensuous chemistry works in your mouth. When you taste marmalade, its sweet and sour elements affect the taste sensors at the front of your tongue. You then experience the bitter sensations in the back. At the same time, floral aromas of citrus oil flood your nose with fragrance. It's a uniquely gratifying experience.

I have enjoyed experimenting with these taste elements in the marmalades. That's one reason why there are two recipes for Pink Grapefruit Marmalade and three for Orange Marmalade (see index). Because bitter oranges are hard to find in the United States, I have added lemons to the orange marmalades to heighten their sour and bitter elements. When a recipe calls for oranges, select a navel or Valencia orange rather than a thin-skinned juice orange. Keep in mind that the white inner peel is the principal source of pectin.

These recipe variations on a single fruit theme demonstrate which technical aspects of making marmalade can be modified and how. You will immediately notice, for example, that some recipes take two days to make, and others take three days. This extended time frame permits flavor exchanges during several cooking periods.

The fruit in all these recipes is diluted in an equal volume of water, which will become the jelly of the marmalade. The water is flavored by the fruit juices and oils during cooking. Its presence, in turn, softens the texture and harsh bitter taste of the peel. This interaction continues as the fruit is cooked and steeped in the water. Some volatile oil is driven off with repeated cooking; flavors also concentrate as the mixture reduces.

As a result of this complex exchange, you will find that a two-day marmalade has a mild jelly with vivid flavor and distinct texture in the fruit pieces. The three-day version enjoys a better-developed jelly flavor and milder fruit bits.

The texture and taste of a marmalade are also affected by the way the fruit is cut and the amount of bitter peel it contains. When the whole citrus fruit is chopped, you are assured a powerful, tangy peel and chewy bits of membrane mixed with a soft juicy pulp. The citrus vitality that is captured in

Pink Grapefruit Marmalade I (see index) can be mellowed by a three-day treatment but never dulled. But recipes where only chunky strips, thin julienne slivers, or grated zest of citrus fruits are reserved, and the fruit is thinly sliced, will be less bitter and more subtle in texture by degrees depending on whether they are cooked over two or three days. Because the pectin-rich inner white peel has been discarded, these marmalades may also require the addition of Apple Pectin Stock to jell (Orange Marmalade II and III; see index).

Although the steel blade of a food processor can dice sections of whole fruit to a fairly fine texture for the zestier marmalades such as Orange Marmalade I (see index), it is unable to slice through the tough peel in citrus fruit without also mauling and extracting juice from the softer membrane and pulp. In some recipes, such as Orange Marmalade II (see index), you have the option of chopping peeled fruit in the processor. However, only good hand tools allow you to adjust cutting pressure for the more delicate job of slicing whole fruits, as in the Lemon Ginger Marmalade (see index), as well as for trimming peel and slicing citrus pulp (Lemon Lime Marmalade; see index). Peeling tools are illustrated in Chapter 2; the properties of a fine knife for trimming peel and slicing fruit are also described in Chapter 2. When careful attention is paid to the texture of citrus peel and pulp, it can become a succulent taste element in your marmalades.

A quick glance through the other marmalade recipes reveals how a wide range of ingredients can produce exciting flavor effects. Some recipes focus on one special citrus fruit, as in the Old-Fashioned Lime Marmalade (see index), or combine only citrus fruits, as in the Mixed Citrus Marmalade (see index). Others call for both citrus and noncitrus fruits, as in the Cranberry Orange Marmalade (see index). Or a marmalade can feature a spice, as does the Lemon Ginger Marmalade (see index). Occasionally even vegetables make an appearance, as in the unexpected Ratatouille Marmalade (see index).

TECHNIQUE FOR MAKING MARMALADE

The flavor of a marmalade is affected by the choice of fruits, the way they are cut, the amount of citrus pectin in them, and the number of times they are cooked. The marmalade technique blends these choices for individual expression with a basically inflexible jelling process. The Old-Fashioned Lime Marmalade (see index) is a good recipe in which to examine the important steps.

On the first day the limes are cut and soaked overnight in water. The amount of peel (pectin) and the texture of the preserve are established by the way the limes have been cut.

On the second day the lime mixture is cooked for 15 minutes, then cooled and steeped overnight. This is the step that makes for a mellow flavor as the hot fruit pieces reabsorb some of the juices and oils they have exuded during cooking.

On the third day the lime mixture is measured for volume and pectin strength.

Two-day marmalade recipes condense the second and third day into one, omitting the second night of steeping. To develop flavor more quickly in a two-day marmalade, some recipes call for cooking the ingredients before steeping, as in the Apple and Onion Marmalade (see index). There are even slight variations on this theme. For example, oranges are cooked alone in Orange Cranberry Marmalade (see index) to activate their pectin and flavor the water so the next day the cranberries can be cooked briefly to guard their plump, whole shape.

You can tell the Old-Fashioned Lime Marmalade has ample pectin because sugar is added cup for cup by volume. When there is insufficient pectin in a marmalade base, you will first reduce the volume of juice as in the recipe for Cinnamon Citrus Marmalade with Apricots (see index). In the Orange Marmalades II and III (see index) you will reduce the liquids and add Pectin Stock before adding the sugar.

After sufficient pectin has been established, cooking marmalade to the jell point is identical to that step in making a jelly. Sugar is measured cup for cup with the fruit mixture. When the quantity is more than 3 cups, the sugar is warmed for 10 minutes in a 250° F. oven. You will add the sugar ½ cup at a time and wait for the liquid to return to the boil before adding more. When all the sugar has been added, let the liquid boil up (you will not be able to stir it down) until it reaches the jell point. This temperature will be 8 degrees above the boiling temperature measured on your thermometer. You will usually reach the jelling temperature within 10-15 minutes and occasionally in 20-30 minutes. In recipes to which Pectin Stock is added you will maintain the boil for a full minute after reaching the jell point.

The recipes specify letting the finished marmalade sit off the heat for 5 minutes. This rest gives the jelly time to begin setting. Stir it briefly at the end of this time to distribute the citrus peel and pulp. They should stay suspended when ladled into jars.

You will use the same procedure for filling and sealing jars as in the jelly recipes:

Sterilize and drain the jars. Fill them to within ½ inch of the rim and cover lightly with plastic wrap until the top sets. Wipe clean the inner rims of the jar so the wax will make good contact with the glass.

Melt the paraffin in its pitcher over hot water. Pour on a layer ⅛-inch thick, tilting and rotating the jar to seal the edges and form an even coating. Check the seal when it has cooled and add another layer if you see any bubbles or cracks.

When the jars have all cooled to room temperature, label and attach snap-on lids. Store as directed in each recipe.

Pink Grapefruit Marmalade I

Zesty is the best way to describe this quick marmalade. The bitter finish results from the presence of inner white peel that is cooked only once. Try this intensely flavorful preserve on English Muffins with Yogurt, Buckwheat Muffins, or Risen Biscuits (see index).

2 pink grapefruits (1¾-2 pounds)
Water
5 cups sugar

Day 1

Quarter the grapefruit and slice each section into ½-inch-thick wedges. Cut these pieces into coarse dice by hand or chop the pieces from 1 grapefruit at a time with rapid on-and-off motions in a food processor until the peel and pulp are cut the size of lima beans.

Measure the fruit pieces and combine them with an equal volume of cool water in a mixing bowl. Cover the bowl with plastic wrap. Leave it to stand at room temperature overnight.

Day 2

Pour the marmalade mix into a heavy, nonreactive 4-quart pot and bring to a boil. Reduce it to 4 cups. During the last 10 minutes of this reduction, warm the sugar in a preheated 250° F. oven.

Stir warm sugar into the reduced grapefruit mixture ½ cup at a time, allowing it to return to the boil before adding more. Keep marmalade at a boil until it reaches the jell point, which is 8 degrees higher than the boiling temperature measured on your thermometer. This will take about 10 minutes. (Recipe continues on following page.)

Off the heat, skim foam from the surface and let the marmalade sit in the pot for 5 minutes. Stir down the fruit pieces and pour into hot, sterilized jelly jars to within ½ inch of the lips. Cover the jars lightly with plastic until the top surfaces set.

Melt paraffin in its pitcher over hot water. Wipe the inner rims of the jars clean. Pour on a ⅛-inch-thick layer of wax. Rotate and tilt it a bit to seal the edges and evenly coat the surface.

Let the jars cool to room temperature overnight before attaching snap-on lids, labeling, and storing in a cool, dark, dry spot.

YIELD: 5 cups

Pink Grapefruit Marmalade II

A three-day grapefruit marmalade that has been steeped and cooked twice develops a mellow blend of its sweet, sour, and bitter elements.

This preserve tastes wonderful on Tea Brack and Oatmeal Muffins (see index).

2 pink grapefruit (1¾-2 pounds)
Water
5 cups sugar

Day 1

Quarter the grapefruit and slice each section into ½-inch-thick wedges. Cut the pieces into coarse dice by hand or chop the pieces from one grapefruit at a time with rapid on-and-off motions in a food processor until the peel and pulp are cut the size of a lima bean.

Measure the fruit pieces and combine them with an equal volume of cool water in a mixing bowl. Cover the bowl with plastic wrap. Let it stand at room temperature overnight.

Day 2

Pour the marmalade mix into a heavy, nonreactive 4-quart pot and bring to a boil. Reduce the heat to simmer and cook for 10 minutes. Let this cool to room temperature in the pot, cover, and let stand overnight at room temperature.

Day 3

Bring the mixture to a boil and reduce to 4 cups. During the last 10 minutes of this reduction, warm the sugar in a preheated 250° F. oven.

Stir the warm sugar into the reduced grapefruit mixture ½ cup at a time, allowing it to return to the boil before adding more. Keep marmalade at a boil until it reaches the jell point, which is 8 degrees higher than the boiling temperature measured on your thermometer. This will take about 5 minutes.

Off the heat, skim foam from the surface and let marmalade sit in the pot for 5 minutes. Stir down the fruit pieces and pour into hot, sterilized jelly jars to within ½ inch of the lips. Cover the jars lightly with plastic wrap until the top surfaces set.

Melt paraffin in its pitcher over hot water. Wipe the inner rims of the jars clean. Pour on a ⅛-inch-thick layer of wax. Rotate and tilt it a bit to seal the edges and evenly coat the surface.

Let the jars cool to room temperature overnight before attaching snap-on lids and storing in a cool, dark, dry spot.

YIELD: 6 cups

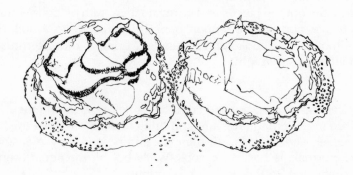

Orange Cranberry Marmalade

A preserve rich in oranges and cranberries comes in handy for many occasions, from Thanksgiving through the Christmas holiday. It makes a memorably sweet-sour filling for a dessert tart garnished with fresh orange slices. You could use it as a relish with turkey or ham. Wouldn't it also make a delightful holiday gift?

Butter Pecan Muffins and Cream Scones (see index) are my favorite breads with this preserve.

3 medium navel oranges (1 pound)
2 cups water
1 pound cranberries
4 cups sugar

Day 1

Finely chop 1 orange, peel intact. (Cut it into eight pieces and chop with rapid on-and-off motions in the food processor.) Cut the peel from the other 2 oranges, halve them, and thinly slice.

Measure the orange pieces and combine them with an equal volume of water in a heavy, nonreactive 4-quart pan. Bring mixture to a boil, reduce heat to a simmer, and cook for 15 minutes. Cool to room temperature, cover, and let stand overnight.

Day 2

Pick over and discard bruised cranberries before weighing them. Rinse them and add to the orange mixture and bring to a boil. Reduce the heat to a simmer, cover, and cook for 10 minutes, stirring regularly. Measure and reduce this marmalade base to 4 cups. While boiling the liquid, warm the sugar in a preheated 250° F. oven for 10 minutes.

Stir in the warm sugar ½ cup at a time, allowing it to return to the boil before adding more. Continue to cook until the marmalade reaches the jell point, which is 8 degrees above the boiling temperature measured on your thermometer. This will take about 5 minutes.

Off the heat, skim foam from the marmalade and let sit in the pan for

5 minutes. Stir down the fruit pieces and pour into hot, sterilized jelly jars to within ½ inch of the lips. Cover the jars loosely with plastic wrap until the tops set.

Melt the paraffin in its pitcher over water. Wipe the inner rims of the jars clean and pour on a ⅛-inch-thick layer of wax. Rotate and tilt the jars to seal the edges and evenly coat the surface.

Let the jars come to room temperature overnight before attaching snap-on lids, labeling, and storing in a cool, dark, dry spot.

YIELD: 5 cups

Orange Marmalade I

This is the first and most assertive of three orange marmalade recipes. That's because it is quick, allowing little time for sweet, sour, and bitter flavors to blend. I enjoy it most on warm breads with contrasting flavors and scents, such as the Apple Cinnamon Muffins and Banana Bran Muffins (see index).

4 medium navel oranges (1½ pounds)
2 medium lemons (8 ounces)
Water
3¾ cups sugar

Day 1

Quarter oranges lengthwise. Cut each quarter in half through the middle to remove seeds. Cut these pieces into coarse dice by hand or chop them to the size of lima beans in two batches, using rapid on-and-off motions, in a food processor.

Treat the lemons the same way. (Process all pieces at once to a slightly finer consistency than oranges.)

Measure the combined fruit pulp and pour it into a mixing bowl. Add an equal volume of cool water. Cover the bowl with plastic wrap and let it stand at room temperature overnight.

(Recipe continues on following page.)

Day 2

Bring the marmalade base to a boil in a heavy, nonreactive 4-quart pot. Reduce heat to an active simmer and cook, uncovered, until it is reduced to 4 cups.

During the last 10 minutes of this reduction, warm the sugar in a preheated 250° F. oven for 10 minutes.

Begin adding the sugar ½ cup at a time to the reduced mixture, allowing it to return to the boil after every addition before adding more. Allow the marmalade to boil until it reaches the jell temperature, which is 8 degrees above the boiling temperature measured on your thermometer. This will take 10-15 minutes.

Off the heat, skim the surface and let marmalade sit in the pot for 5 minutes. Stir down the fruit pieces and pour the marmalade into hot, sterilized jelly jars to within ½ inch of the lips. Cover jars loosely with plastic wrap until the top surfaces set.

Warm the paraffin in its pitcher over hot water. Wipe the inner edges of the rims clean. Pour on a ⅛-inch-thick layer of wax, tilting and rotating the jar to seal the edges and evenly coat the surface.

Let jars cool to room temperature overnight. Cover with snap-on lids, label, and store in a cool, dark, dry storage place.

This marmalade should age a week to allow peel to soften in its jelly.

YIELD: 4 cups

Orange Marmalade II

In this second of three marmalade recipes much of the bitter inner peel from the oranges and lemons is discarded. As a result, the preserve has to be reduced and supplemented with Pectin Stock before it will jell.

This is sweeter than Orange Marmalade I but more tangy than Orange Marmalade III (see index).

4 medium navel oranges (1½ pounds)
2 medium lemons (8 ounces)
Water
1½ cups Pectin Stock (see index)
3½ cups sugar

Day 1

Use a stripper tool (illustrated in Chapter 3) to trim most of the outer peel from the oranges and lemons. Reserve this. Cut off and discard the remaining inner white pith. Quarter oranges and lemons lengthwise and cut these pieces crosswise to remove seeds. Cut these pieces into coarse dice by hand or chop them to the size of lima beans with 5-6 rapid on-and-off motions in the food processor, processing a dozen sections at a time.

Measure the combined strips and pulp. Pour this into a bowl and cover with an equal volume of water. Spread plastic wrap over the top and let it stand at room temperature overnight.

Day 2

Pour marmalade base into a heavy, nonreactive 4-quart pot and bring to a boil. Regulate the heat to a steady simmer and cook, uncovered, until it is reduced to 2½ cups. During the last 10 minutes, warm the sugar in a 250° F. oven.

Stir the Pectin Stock into the orange mixture and bring it back to a boil. Add the warm sugar ½ cup at a time, allowing the pot to return to the boil before adding more. Let the marmalade boil up until it reaches the jell temperature, which is 8 degrees higher than the boiling temperature measured on your thermometer. This will take 10 to 12 minutes. Maintain the boil for a full minute after reaching the jell point.

Off the heat, skim off the foam and let marmalade sit in the pot for 5 minutes. Stir down the fruit pieces and pour into hot, sterilized jelly jars to within ½ inch of the lips.

Cover the filled jars loosely with plastic wrap until the fruit pieces stay suspended in the marmalade when stirred down and the tops begin to set.

Melt paraffin in its pitcher over hot water. Wipe clean the inner rims of the jars. Pour a ⅛-inch-thick layer of wax over the marmalade, tilting and rotating the jars slightly to seal the edges and evenly coat the surface.

Allow the jars to cool to room temperature overnight before attaching snap-on lids, labeling, and storing in a cool, dark, dry spot.

YIELD: 4 cups

Orange Marmalade III

Here is the most fruity marmalade in the set of three. Since virtually all of the bitter pith in the peel has been eliminated, it is closer to being a preserve than a marmalade.

I use it with many different breads because so many are flattered by the mellowed flavor of oranges. Zucchini Bread, Tea Brack, Butter Pecan Muffins, and Grapenuts Muffins (see index) are examples.

4 medium navel oranges (1 ½ pounds)
2 medium lemons (8 ounces)
Water
1 ½ cups Pectin Stock (see index)
2¾ cups sugar

Day 1

Use a vegetable peeler (illustrated in Chapter 2) to strip the thin outer peel from the oranges and lemons. Slice these into thin pieces ⅛ inch wide. Cut the remaining white pith from the fruits and discard it. Quarter the fruits lengthwise, removing seeds as needed. Cut pieces into coarse dice by hand or chop into bits the size of lima beans with rapid on-and-off motions in a food processor.

Measure the combined slices and zest, pour them into a bowl, and cover with an equal volume of water. Spread plastic wrap over the top and let this mixture sit overnight at room temperature.

Day 2

Pour the marmalade base into a heavy, nonreactive 4-quart pot and bring to a boil. Regulate the heat for a steady simmer and cook, uncovered, until it reduces to 2 cups.

Stir in the Pectin Stock and return liquid to a boil. Add sugar ½ cup at a time, allowing the mixture to return to the boil before adding more. Let the marmalade boil after the sugar is added until it reaches the jell temperature, which is 8 degrees above the boiling temperature measured on your thermometer. This will take about 10 minutes. Maintain the boil for a full minute after reaching the jell point.

Off the heat, skim off any scum and let marmalade sit in the pot for 5 minutes. Stir down the fruit pieces and pour into hot, sterilized jelly jars to within ½ inch of the lips. Loosely cover the jars with plastic wrap until fruit pieces stay suspended in the marmalade when stirred down and the tops set.

Melt paraffin in its pitcher over hot water. Wipe clean the inner rims of the jars. Pour on a ⅛-inch-thick layer, tilting and rotating the jars to seal the edges and evenly coat the surface.

Leave the jars at room temperature overnight before sealing with snap-on lids, labeling, and storing in a cool, dry, dark spot.

YIELD: 3¼ cups

Mixed Citrus Marmalade

When you want a subtle blend of your favorite winter fruits, this is the citrus marmalade you are looking for. The strips of peel are colorful and tangy; the jelly is firm and flavorful. It tastes wonderful on a chewy English Muffin (see index).

I have also substituted this preserve for Lemon Marmalade in the Lemon Amaretto Soufflé (see index), using Grand Marnier in place of Amaretto.

1 pink grapefruit (¾ pound)
2 navel oranges (¾ pound)
2 lemons (6 ounces)
Water
3 cups sugar

Day 1

Use a stripper tool (illustrated in Chapter 2) to peel 30 strips 4 inches long from the grapefruit, 24 strips from each orange, and 18 from each lemon. Cut off the remaining peel from all the fruits. Halve them all and thinly slice, removing seeds as you go. (You could alternatively chop the fruit pulp with rapid on and off movements in the food processor. Cut the grapefruit into 8 pieces, the oranges and lemons each into 4 pieces before placing them in the workbowl.)

(Recipe continues on following page.)

Measure the fruit slices with peel strips and combine them with an equal volume of water in a heavy, nonreactive 4-quart pan. Bring the mixture to a boil, reduce the heat to a simmer, and cook, covered, for 15 minutes. Lift the lid to stir every 5 minutes.

Let the pan and its contents cool to room temperature, cover, and let sit overnight.

Day 2

Measure the marmalade base. If there is more than 3 cups, reduce it to 3 cups. Bring to a boil and add sugar ½ cup at a time, returning it to the boil before adding more. Cook until marmalade reaches the jell point, which is 8 degrees above the boiling temperature measured on your thermometer. This will take less than 10 minutes.

Off the heat, skim the foam from the surface and let the marmalade sit in the pan for 5 minutes. Stir down the fruit pieces and pour into hot, sterilized jelly jars to within ½ inch of the lips. Cover the jars loosely with plastic wrap until the tops have set.

Melt paraffin in its pitcher over hot water. Wipe clean the inner rim of each jar and pour on a ⅛-inch-thick layer of wax. Rotate and tilt the jars to seal the edges and evenly coat the surface.

Let jars come to room temperature overnight before attaching snap-on lids, labeling, and storing in a cool, dark, dry spot.

YIELD: 3 cups

Old-Fashioned Lime Marmalade

This recipe is old-fashioned in its unhurried method and its lightly tart taste with a slightly sweet finish. It's perfect for serving at high tea with warm Cream Scones (see index).

1 pound fresh limes
Water
Sugar

Day 1

Peel the zest from the limes with a vegetable peeler (illustrated in Chapter 2) and cut it into thin slices. Cut off and discard the inner white peel. Thinly slice the fruit, removing all seeds. Measure the volume of zest and fruit (about 2 cups). Cover with an equal volume of water and let this mixture stand overnight.

Day 2

Bring lime mixture to a boil in a heavy, nonreactive 4-quart pan. Reduce heat to a simmer and cook steadily for 15 minutes. Let this cool to room temperature and stand overnight.

Day 3

Measure fruit mixture. Warm an equal volume of sugar in a 250° F. oven for 10 minutes. Bring liquid to a boil. Add the sugar ½ cup at a time, allowing the liquid to return to the boil before adding more. Boil until marmalade reaches the jell point, which is 8 degrees above the boiling point measured on your thermometer. This will happen within 10 minutes.

Let the marmalade sit in the pot for 5 minutes. Stir down the fruit pieces and pour the mixture into hot, sterilized jelly jars to within ½ inch of the lips. Cover them loosely with plastic wrap until the tops set.

Melt the paraffin in its pitcher over hot water. Wipe clean the inner rims of the jars. Pour on a ⅛-inch-thick layer of wax, rotating and tilting the jars to seal the edges and evenly coat the surface.

Let the jars cool to room temperature overnight before attaching snap-on lids, labeling, and storing in a cool, dark, dry spot.

YIELD: 3¼ cups

Lemon Lime Marmalade

Limes and lemons offer distinctively different flavors. One cannot be substituted for the other in food or drink without a noticeable alteration in taste. Yet this marmalade proves they are not incompatible. A blend of their unique qualities creates a new and most delicious taste harmony.

Lemon Lime Marmalade is delicious on Zucchini Bread and Whole Wheat English Muffins (see index).

> **8 lemons (2½ pounds)**
> **2 limes (8 ounces)**
> **4 cups water**
> **Sugar**
> **1 cinnamon stick**
> **Additional zest of 2 lemons and 1 lime**

Day 1

Trim the zest from lemons and limes with a vegetable peeler (illustrated in Chapter 3) and cut it into thin strips. Cut off and discard inner white peel and thinly slice the fruits. This should measure about 4 cups combined.

Place fruit in a large bowl and cover with an equal volume of water. Soak fruit overnight.

Day 2

Pour marmalade base into a heavy, nonreactive 4-quart pan, add the cinnamon stick, bring to a boil, reduce heat to a simmer, and cook for 15 minutes. Return to the bowl, cool, cover, and let stand overnight at room temperature again.

Day 3

Measure fruit and liquid and warm an equal volume of sugar in a 250° F. oven for 10 minutes.

Bring mixture to a boil and add sugar ½ cup at a time, waiting for the liquid to return to the boil before adding more. Cook until marmalade reaches the jell point, which is 8 degrees above the boiling temperature measured on your thermometer. This will take about 15 minutes.

Off heat, remove the cinnamon stick. Skim the marmalade of foam. Stir in the zest that has been removed with a zester (illustrated in Chapter 2). Let the marmalade sit for 10 minutes in the pot. Stir down the fruit pieces and ladle mixture into hot, sterilized jelly jars to within ½ inch of the lips. Cover the jars loosely with plastic wrap until the tops have set.

Melt the paraffin in its pitcher over hot water. Wipe clean the inner rim of each jar and cover with a ⅛-inch-thick layer of wax, rotating and tilting it to seal the edges and evenly coat the surface.

Let the marmalade jars cool to room temperature overnight. Cover with snap-on lids, label, and store in a cool, dark, dry spot.

YIELD: 8 cups

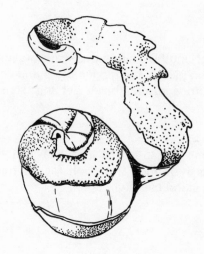

Lemon Ginger Marmalade

The dynamic sensations of sweet, sour, and bitter in lemons combined with hot and aromatic ginger make this a marmalade that wakes up tastebuds and flatters almost any bread. Tea Brack and English Muffins (see index) are particularly good with it.

This preserve can also be transformed into a spectacular Lemon Amaretto Soufflé (see index).

1 pound lemons
3 slices fresh ginger
Water
3½ cups sugar

Day 1

Quarter lemons lengthwise. Remove seeds and thinly slice, leaving peel intact. Measure lemon pieces and ginger slices and cover with an equal volume of cool water in a mixing bowl. Let this stand overnight at room temperature.

Day 2

Bring lemon mixture to a boil in a heavy, nonreactive 4-quart pot. Reduce the heat to a simmer and cook for 15 minutes. Cool to room temperature and let stand overnight again.

Day 3

Measure the marmalade base. Warm an equal volume of sugar in a 250° F. oven for 10 minutes.

Add sugar ½ cup at a time, allowing mixture to return to the boil before adding more. Continue cooking until mixture reaches the jell point, which is 8 degrees above the boiling temperature measured on your thermometer. This will happen within 10 minutes.

Off the heat, skim hot marmalade of foam. Let it sit for 5 minutes in the pot. Stir down the fruit pieces and pour into hot, sterilized jelly jars to within ½ inch of the lips. Cover the jars loosely with plastic wrap until the tops are set.

Melt the paraffin in its pitcher over hot water. Wipe the inside rims of the jars clean. Pour on a ⅛-inch-thick layer of wax, rotating and tilting the jars to seal the edges and evenly coat the surface.

Let the jars cool to room temperature overnight before attaching snap-on lids, labeling, and storing in a cool, dark, dry spot.

YIELD: 4 cups

Cinnamon Citrus Marmalade with Apricots

Dried apricots add a sweet accent and toothsome texture to sour citrus ingredients that is quite pleasing in this marmalade.

This marmalade would taste wonderful on warm Buckwheat Muffins or English Muffins (see index).

6 ounces dried apricots
1 pink grapefruit (1 pound)
1 navel orange (½ pound)
1 lemon (¼ pound)
3½ cups water
1 4-inch stick cinnamon
4 cups sugar

Day 1

Coarsely chop the apricots. Measure them and cover with an equal volume of boiling water in a 2-quart mixing bowl.

Trim the zest from the citrus fruits with a vegetable peeler (illustrated in Chapter 2) and cut into thin strips. Cut off and discard the remaining inner white peel. Quarter and slice the fruits, discarding seeds. Add these to the steeping apricots and add cool water to just cover. Let this mixture sit, covered, overnight at room temperature.

Day 2

Pour fruits and liquid into a heavy, nonreactive 4-quart saucepan. Add cinnamon stick and bring to a boil. Reduce heat to a simmer and cook gently for 10 minutes or until the mixture measures 4 cups. Let this cool, cover, and let stand overnight again at room temperature.

Day 3

Warm sugar in a 250° F. oven for 10 minutes. Bring marmalade base to a boil and simmer 5 minutes. Add sugar ½ cup at a time, allowing the mixture to return to the boil before adding more. Continue cooking until it reaches the jell point, which is 8 degrees above the boiling point measured on your thermometer. This will take 5-10 minutes.

Off the heat, skim off foam and remove cinnamon stick. Let the marmalade sit in the pot for 5 minutes. Stir down the fruit pieces and pour into hot, sterilized jelly jars to within ½ inch of the lips. Cover the jars loosely with plastic wrap until the tops have set.

Melt the paraffin in its own pitcher over hot water. Wipe the inner rims of the jars clean. Pour on a ⅛-inch-thick layer of wax, rotating and tilting the jars to seal the edges and evenly coat the surface.

Let the jars cool to room temperature overnight before attaching the snap-on lids, labeling, and storing in a cool, dark, dry spot.

YIELD: 5 cups

Red Pepper Marmalade

Red pepper's natural sweetness lends a distinctive taste to the blended citrus ingredients. No spices are specified here, but ginger or cinnamon, even bay leaves make an interesting addition.

Cornmeal Muffins and English Muffins with Yogurt (see index) would add texture and an interesting scent to this marmalade, eaten warm for breakfast or with soup for supper.

> 6 large red peppers (l¼-1½ pounds)
> 3 navel oranges (1-1½ pounds)
> 2 lemons (8 ounces)
> 4 cups water
> ½ cup Pectin Stock (see index)
> 4 cups sugar
> Optional seasonings: 3 slices fresh ginger, 1 4″ cinnamon stick, *or*
>   2 bay leaves

Day 1

Rinse peppers. Halve them; remove stem, seeds, and membrane. Thinly slice them.

Halve and slice 1 orange, leaving on the peel. Cut off the peel, halve, and thinly slice the remaining 2 oranges.

Quarter 1 lemon. Cut off the pith at the wedge edges to remove seeds. Thinly slice fruit with the peel on. Squeeze the juice from the other lemon.

Combine pepper slices, oranges, lemon slices, lemon juice, and an optional seasoning with water in a heavy, nonreactive 5-quart pan. Bring liquid to a boil, reduce heat to an active simmer, and cook for 15 minutes. Let mixture cool to room temperature, cover, and let sit overnight.

Day 2

Bring marmalade base to a boil and reduce to 4 cups. While this reduction is going on, warm sugar for 10 minutes in a preheated 250° F. oven.

Add the Pectin Stock to the reduced mixture and bring to a boil. Stir in the warm sugar ½ cup at a time, returning it to a boil before adding more. Continue to boil until it reaches the jell point, which is 8 degrees above the boiling temperature measured on your thermometer. This will take about 10 minutes. Maintain the boil for a full minute after reaching the jell point.

Let the marmalade sit in the pot for 5 minutes. Remove the seasoning pieces, stir down the pepper pieces and ladle the marmalade into hot, sterilized jelly jars to within ½ inch of the lips. Cover the jars loosely with plastic wrap until the tops have set.

Melt the paraffin in its pitcher over water. Wipe clean the inner rims of the jars and cover with ⅛ inch of wax, rotating and tilting them to seal the edges and evenly coat the surface.

Let the jars cool to room temperature overnight before attaching snap-on lids, labeling, and storing in a cool, dark, dry spot.

YIELD: 5 cups

Apple and Onion Marmalade

Apples and onions are frequently paired as a garnish for pork, liver, and cabbage dishes, and they complement each other here. Lemon seemed the natural citrus partner with them in a marmalade.

You'll find this textured preserve delicious with Buckwheat Muffins or Grapenuts Muffins (see index) and as a condiment with cold pork or roast beef.

2 lemons (8 ounces)
3 medium Granny Smith apples (1 pound)
2 small onions (8 ounces)
Water
1 cup Pectin Stock (see index)
4 cups sugar

Day 1

Use a vegetable peeler (illustrated in Chapter 2) to remove the outer colored peel from the lemons. Slice these strips into thin strips ⅛ inch wide. Cut off and discard any remaining peel and the white inner pith. Halve the lemons and thinly slice them, removing seeds as necessary. Place the lemon strips and slices in a heavy, nonreactive 4-quart pan and cover with a quart of water.

Peel, quarter, and core the apples. Slice the quarters into thirds lengthwise and thinly slice horizontally into wedges. (They may be chopped into coarse dice with rapid on-and-off motions in the food processor.) Drop the apple pieces in the lemon mixture as soon as they are sliced.

Peel and thinly slice the onions. Add them to the apples and lemons. Pour on additional water to cover the mixture. Bring to a boil, reduce the heat to a simmer, and cook, uncovered, for 15 minutes. Let the mixture cool to room temperature, cover, and let sit overnight at room temperature.

Day 2

Add the Pectin Stock to the marmalade base and bring it to a boil. Reduce it over high heat to 4 cups. While this reduction is going on, warm the sugar on a baking sheet in a preheated 250° F. oven.

Stir in the warm sugar ½ cup at a time, waiting for the mixture to return to the boil before adding more. Allow the mixture to boil and reach 218° F. This may take as long as 15 minutes. Give the marmalade the cold plate test to double-check for the jell. Chill a plate in the freezer for 3 minutes. Add a tablespoon of marmalade and return it to the freezer for a minute. If the chilled preserve ripples when you push a finger into it, it is beginning to jell. Maintain the boil for a full minute after you establish the jell.

Off the heat, skim foam from the surface and let the marmalade sit for 5 minutes. Stir down the fruit pieces and pour into hot, sterilized jelly jars to within ½ inch of the lips. Cover the jars loosely with plastic wrap until the floating pieces stay suspended when stirred down.

Melt the paraffin in its pitcher over hot water. Wipe clean the inner rims of the jars. Pour on a ⅛-inch-thick layer of wax, tilting and rotating the jars to seal the edges and evenly coat the surface. Allow the jars to remain at room temperature overnight before attaching snap-on lids, labeling, and storing.

YIELD: about 4 cups

Lime Zucchini Marmalade

Slim, firm zucchini no more than 6 inches long are the best for grating into this mild and fragrant preserve. The dark green and white flecks they leave suspended in jelly will be most tender and flattering to the citrus fruits and seasonings.

Lime Zucchini Marmalade is a delicious addition to a batch of Oatmeal Muffins or Risen Biscuits (see index).

1 pound grated zucchini
3 limes (½ pound), thinly sliced
Juice of 1 lemon
3 cups water
1 bay leaf
1 3-inch stick cinnamon
2 cups Pectin Stock (see index)
3½ cups sugar

Day 1

Combine grated squash, lime slices, lemon juice, water, bay leaf, and cinnamon in a heavy, nonreactive 4-quart pan. Bring to a boil and cook, uncovered, at a slow simmer for 15 minutes.

Cool this mixture to room temperature, cover, and let sit overnight.

Day 2

Add the Pectin Stock and reduce this mixture to 4 cups.

During the last 10 minutes of the reducing period, warm the sugar in a 250° F. oven. Add warm sugar to the liquid ½ cup at a time, returning the liquid to the boil before adding more. Cook at medium-high until the marmalade reaches the jell temperature, which is 8 degrees above the boiling temperature measured on your thermometer. This will take up to 30 minutes. Maintain the boil for a full minute after reaching the jell point.

Pick out the bay leaf and cinnamon. Let the marmalade sit for 5 minutes. Stir down the fruit pieces and ladle the mixture into hot, sterilized jars to within ½ inch of the lips. Cover the jars loosely with plastic wrap until the top has set.

Melt the paraffin in its pitcher over hot water. Wipe clean the inner rims of the jars. Pour on a ⅛-inch-thick layer of wax, rotating and tilting the jars to seal the edges and evenly coat the surface.

When marmalade has cooled to room temperature, cover jars with snap-on lids, label, and store in a cool, dark, dry spot.

YIELD: 4 cups

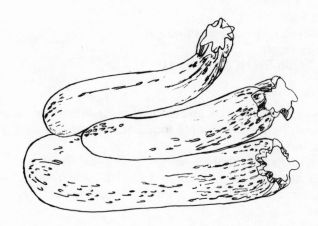

Orange Zucchini Marmalade

Small, tender zucchini sliced in thin rings is as wonderful with oranges as in the Lime Zucchini Marmalade. This time the texture is bolder and so is the taste after the introduction of tangy sections of fresh ginger root.

Why not try this preserve with Zucchini Bread (see index) for more taste of a good thing?

1 pound small zucchini
½ pound navel oranges (1 orange)
Juice of 1 lime
4 cups water
3 quarter-sized pieces fresh ginger
3½ cups sugar
1 cup Pectin Stock (see index)

Day 1

Trim ends of the zucchini and thinly slice. Quarter the oranges and trim off enough pith holding segments together to remove seeds. Thinly slice these pieces with peel intact.

Combine zucchini, orange pieces, lime juice, water, and ginger in a heavy, nonreactive 5-quart pan. Bring liquid to a boil, reduce the heat to a simmer, and cook slowly for 20 minutes. Let mixture cool, cover, and let sit overnight.

Day 2

Measure and reduce the mixture to 3 cups. Warm sugar for 10 minutes in a 250° F. oven during the last 10 minutes of the reduction. Stir Pectin Stock into the pot. Bring to a boil and add sugar ½ cup at a time, returning liquid to a boil before adding more. Continue to boil until the mixture reaches the jell temperature, which is 8 degrees above the boiling temperature measured on your thermometer. This will take about 20 minutes. Maintain the boil for a full minute after reaching the jell point.

Off the heat, remove ginger slices. Let the marmalade sit in the pot for 5 minutes. Stir down the fruit pieces and ladle mixture into hot, sterilized jars to within ½ inch of the lips. Cover jars loosely with plastic wrap until the tops have set.

Melt the paraffin in its pitcher over hot water. Wipe clean the inner rims of the jars and pour on a ⅛-inch-thick coat of wax, rotating and tilting the jars to seal the edges and evenly coat the surface.

When marmalade has cooled to room temperature, attach snap-on lids, label, and keep in a cool, dark, dry, place.

YIELD: 4½ cups

Citrus and Green Pepper Marmalade

The summer peppers, winter citrus, and festive seasonings make this marmalade a yearlong favorite on brunch buffets and barbecue picnics. It will taste great on fresh-baked Risen Biscuits and Cornmeal Muffins (see index).

3 navel oranges (1 pound)
2 green peppers (8-10 ounces)
1 lemon
5 cups water
Bouquet garni: 3 cloves, 6 fennel seeds, 1 slice fresh ginger
4 cups sugar

Day 1

Quarter oranges and thinly slice with peels on. Quarter the green peppers, remove seeds, stems, and membranes, and thinly slice.

Combine fruit and vegetable slices in a bowl, cover with cool water, and let stand overnight.

Day 2

Pour mixture into a heavy, nonreactive 4-quart pan. Add the spices tied in cheesecloth with cotton twine and bring to a boil. Reduce heat to a simmer and cook for 15 minutes. Cool the mixture and return it to the bowl. Cover the top with plastic wrap and let stand overnight.

Day 3

Warm the sugar for 10 minutes in a 250° F. oven. Bring the marmalade base to a boil and reduce it to 4 cups. Add sugar ½ cup at a time, waiting for the marmalade to return to the boil before adding more. Continue to boil until it reaches the jell point, which is 8 degrees above the boiling temperature measured on your thermometer. This will take 10-15 minutes.

Off the heat, remove spice bag and skim off any foam. Let the marmalade sit for 5 minutes in the pot. Stir down the fruit pieces and pour marmalade into hot, sterilized jelly jars to within ½ inch of the lips. Cover the jars loosely with plastic wrap until the tops set.

Melt the paraffin in its pitcher over hot water. Wipe the inner rims of the jars clean. Pour on a ⅛-inch-thick layer of the wax, rotating and tilting the jars to seal the edges and evenly coat the surface.

Let jars cool to room temperature overnight. Attach snap-on lids, label, and store in a cool, dark, dry spot.

YIELD: 5 cups

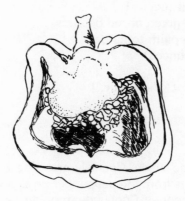

Ratatouille Marmalade

A classic ratatouille blend of zucchini, tomato, onion, and green pepper becomes a rich marmalade balanced between sweet and sour ingredients. The lemons provide a tart taste that is brought into equilibrium by the sugar.

This is a preserve meant for a serious breakfast table or a picnic spread and can be served with steamy hot Risen Biscuits and Buckwheat English Muffins (see index). A vegetable marmalade is also good with cold leftover roasts and spicy sausages.

4 ounces onion
12 ounces small zucchini
4 ounces sweet green or red peppers
8 ounces Italian plum tomatoes
3 lemons (12 ounces)
1 quart water
1 cup Pectin Stock (see index)
Sugar
4 teaspoons fresh lemon juice

Day 1

Peel and slice the onion. Coarsely grate the zucchini. Remove stem, seeds, and membranes from the pepper before slicing. Dip the tomatoes in boiling water for 30 seconds. Cool under running water and slip off the skin. Halve each tomato and press the seeds through a sieve, reserving the juices. Halve and thinly slice 2 lemons with peels intact. Squeeze and strain the juice from the third lemon. Combine these ingredients in a heavy, nonreactive 5-quart pot with the water.

Bring mixture to a boil, regulate to a simmer, and cook, uncovered, for 15 minutes. Let this cool to room temperature, cover it, and let stand overnight.

Day 2

The next day, pour in the Pectin Stock and measure this marmalade base. Warm an equal volume of sugar in a 250°F. oven for 5 minutes.

Bring mixture to a boil. Add the warm sugar ½ cup at a time, waiting for the mixture to return to the boil before adding more sugar. Pour in additional lemon juice and boil hard until the marmalade reaches the jell point, which is 8 degrees above the boiling temperature measured on your thermometer. This will take 15-20 minutes. Maintain the boil for a full minute after reaching the jell point.

Skim any foam from the surface and let the marmalade sit for 5 minutes in the pot. Stir down the fruit pieces and ladle marmalade into hot, sterilized jelly jars to within ½ inch of the lips. Cover them lightly with plastic wrap until the tops are set.

Melt the paraffin in its pitcher over hot water. Wipe clean the inner rims of the jars. Pour on a ⅛-inch-thick layer of wax, turning and tilting it to seal the edges and evenly coat the surface.

Let the jars sit to cool overnight at room temperature. Cover jars with snap-on lids, label, and store in a cool, dark, dry spot.

YIELD: 7 cups

7

PRESERVES

So far I have been using the word *preserves* both generally and specifically. Now is the time to clarify the definition of a fruit preserve as a specific technique within the larger world of fruit preserving.

Ever since the Romans stored figs in honey, fruit preserves have been synonymous with sweetened produce that is stored from one season to the next. This basic association relates all the techniques in this book to one another. The idea that a fruit preserve should consist of whole fruits and berries suspended in a sugar syrup distinguishes a specific cooking process, the one we are analyzing here.

The traditional process for making preserves is one of multiple poachings. Fruits are cooked and cooled in a sugar syrup so that the juices they exude when heated are reabsorbed as they cool. Repeated cooking and cooling gradually mingle juices and syrup to the point where the density of the juices inside the fruit is the same as that of the surrounding liquid, causing the fruit to hang suspended in the poaching medium.

When I began this project, I knew I would have to devise a modern fruit preserve technique, one that dispensed with the tooth-itching sweetness of this sugar-saturated process. I worked on a method that developed flavor elements and reduced sugar content in a manner consistent with the sensitive fruit jells and jam reductions in previous chapters.

My solution is to cook fruit, strain its juices, and make a natural jelly in which to steep the strained fruit pieces. The jelly formula I have developed is both flavorful enough and dense enough to support the fruit pieces.

137

This new preserve technique will give your preserves a rich, intense taste and a sensuous texture. Since recipes call for only three to four pounds of fruit, the jelly yield is small. This means that the preserve is thick with fruit. The taste of a tablespoon of the Strawberry Preserves (see index), for example, makes you feel you are eating a whole pint in one bite.

There are five major steps to this new technique for preserves. First the fruits are gently cooked or baked to withdraw juices without destroying their texture. Next the juices are strained and measured. In the third step juices are cooked with sugar into a jelly. The fruit pieces are then allowed to mix and plump up in the jelly. A final cooking concentrates the preserve near or at the jell point.

You will see that there is little room for expressive intervention once cooking begins, since fruit texture, sugar volume, and the finished consistency of preserves are all predetermined. The pleasure for creative cooks lies in mixing fruit flavors and seasonings.

I have discovered, for example, that the fruits most appropriate for jelly (those with high pectin content) make quite tasty preserve bases for low-pectin fruits. My favorites include Pear and Grape Preserves and its cousin, Apple Grape Preserves (see index). The Apple Red Raspberry Preserves (see index) is another example. Red currant juice is spectacular in the Cherry Preserves with Cassis (see index). But it's not essential to combine high- and low-pectin fruits all the time. In the Pear Preserves with Pernod (see index), for example, the scent of Pernod with the fruit was developed at the expense of a firm jell, yielding what I believe is a much more interesting flavor.

TECHNIQUE FOR MAKING PRESERVES

The 1½-hour period you will need to make a fruit preserve is distinguished by an easy rhythm of alternating work and rest times. You will want to be attentive while the fruit is cooking, but you can rest or even put the process on hold while the fruits are straining and again when they are steeping in hot jelly.

Since there are recipe variations in each of the five preserving steps, it is easier to talk about each part separately than to follow a single recipe from beginning to end.

For example, in almost all recipes where preserves are started over direct heat, a small amount of water is added to the fruit to prevent it from sticking to the pot and breaking down while rendering juice. The single exception is the Strawberry Preserves (see index), where you will find specific directions for softening the berries in a pan on the range. In a few berry recipes where the fruit is baked this additional water was not needed. The one radical departure from this initial cooking procedure is found in the Three-Onion Preserve (see index), in which you cook onion slices in Apple Pectin Stock. This recipe will serve as a prototype for a vegetable preserve.

After this initial cooking the fruit is strained for 15 minutes. Solid pieces are reserved while the juice is measured for volume and pectin strength. I have been careful to check the pectin levels in each recipe so the juices will jell quickly in the next step. Some juices have to be reduced to concentrate pectin, such as the Four-Berry Preserves (see index). The Tropical Pineapple Preserves (see index) is among those that call for reduction and a supplement of Pectin Stock. Preserves made with pectin-rich fruits or juices like grape or red currant will be ready for the next step after straining without further cooking or additions.

The ratio of sugar to strained juice will be one-to-one by volume for the jelly-making step. Bring juices to the boil and stir in the sugar ½ cup at a time, allowing the liquid to return to the boil after each addition. The Red Raspberry Preserves (see index) is the only recipe that will require more than 3 cups of sugar, an amount that warrants warming it first. Since these are small fruit juice volumes, you may have to tip the pan to collect enough juice for an accurate temperature reading. The juices will reach the jell point within 5 minutes in most recipes and in no longer than 10 minutes in all the recipes.

Lemon juice is frequently added in this third step to enhance the acid element that serves as a catalyst in the jelling process. This slight bit of acidity is also a welcome flavor contrast.

After the juices have reached the jell point, you will return the cooked fruits to the pot. They will imbibe the jelly and swell up to their formerly plump profiles in 15 minutes.

A second cooking to reestablish the jell is the final step in making preserves. In a few recipes a bit more lemon juice is added along with a small amount of sugar. These late additions are intended to jell the small amount of extra juice extracted during this second cooking. This reduction is limited to 10 minutes with few exceptions. The Three-Onion Preserves (see index) may cook for an additional 2 minutes, and the Strawberry Blackberry Preserve (see index) as long as another 5 minutes.

Finished preserve temperatures usually fall between 210° F. and

220° F. This wide range reflects the presence of fruit pieces in the preserves; the more dense the fruit mixture, the lower the temperature will be. For example, Apple Red Raspberry Preserves (see index) are so thick that their finished temperature reaches only 204 degrees, though they cool to a firm jell.

Do not extend cooking time beyond that suggested in the recipe, even if the preserve has not reached the proper temperature. Lengthy cooking drains flavor and increases the possibility that the preserve will stick to the bottom of the pot. The taste and aroma of scorched fruit will quickly pervade the entire pot, ruining the unburned portions as well as the bottom.

You can use very loose fruit preserves as ice cream bases or toppings. They can also be diluted with sugar syrup to use as a sauce or with cream to be frozen into ice cream.

Follow the same procedure for pouring and sealing your preserves in quilted, screw-cap jars as that explained in the introduction to Chapter 4. Ladle the finished preserves into hot, sterilized jars to within ⅛ inch of the lips. Wipe clean the rims for good contact with the sterile lids. Tightly screw on the threaded caps and either invert briefly for a quick seal or cook in a boiling water bath, submerged by 1 inch, for 10 minutes.

Allow the jars to cool to room temperature on a rack overnight. Label and store in a cool, dry, dark cellar or basement until eaten. Refrigerate preserves after opening.

Italian Plum Preserves

The soft flesh of Italian plums has a sweet rather nondescript taste. The tart and fragrant flavor that lies in its thin dark skin is developed in this recipe.

Zucchini Bread and Oatmeal Muffins (see index) are my favorite bread partners for this preserve.

3 pounds Italian plums, quartered and pitted
1 cup water
Sugar
1½ tablespoons fresh lemon juice

Combine plum pieces with water in a heavy, nonreactive 5-quart pan. Bring water to a boil, reduce heat to a steady simmer, cover, and cook for 20 minutes.

Strain juices for 15 minutes and measure. Set aside an equal amount of sugar. Bring juices to a boil, pour in 1 tablespoon lemon juice, and begin adding sugar ½ cup at a time, allowing the mixture to return to the boil before adding more. Continue cooking until the liquid reaches the jell point, which is 8 degrees above the boiling point measured on your thermometer. This will take 5-10 minutes.

Off the heat, stir the plum quarters into the hot jelly and steep for 15 minutes.

Return preserves to a boil. Stir in ½ tablespoon lemon juice and ½ cup sugar. Boil for 10 minutes, stirring frequently, as the liquids reduce and the temperature rises to 215°F.

Off the heat, skim off foam and fill hot, sterilized jars to within ⅛ inch of the lips. Wipe the rims clean, attach new lids, and screw the caps on tightly. Invert the jars briefly for a quick vacuum seal or process in a boiling water bath, submerged by 1 inch, for 10 minutes.

YIELD: 4½ cups

Blackberry Ginger Preserves

The dark, toothsome blackberry makes a spectacular preserve, full of sweet-sour contrast and the fragrance of wilderness. I have added ginger's warm sensations and spicy aroma for emphasis.

Blackberries and buckwheat are a favorite combination of mine. You could use either the blini or muffin recipe (see index). If you like the meaty pulp of this berry and its crunchy seeds, spread it on English Muffins (see index) and enjoy a delicious chewing experience. This preserve will also appear again as a sauce for fresh pears.

3 pounds blackberries (see note)
1 slice fresh ginger (size of a quarter)
Sugar
Zest of 2 lemons

Preheat the oven to 350° F. Bake the berries in a heavy, nonreactive 5-quart pot, covered, for 40 minutes.

Strain off juices for 20 minutes.

Measure blackberry juice and set aside 1 cup sugar for every cup of juice.

Bring the juice to a boil with the slice of ginger root in a 4-quart pan. Stir in the sugar ½ cup at a time, allowing the pot to return to the boil between additions. Continue to boil until it reaches the jell point, which is 8 degrees above the boiling temperature measured on your thermometer. This will take about 5 minutes.

Off the heat, stir the fruit pieces into the hot jelly to steep for 15 minutes.

Bring the blackberry preserve to a boil with the lemon zest removed with a zester (illustrated in Chapter 2) and cook until it reaches 218° F. If it has not reached this temperature in 5 minutes, add another ½ cup sugar. Cook preserves another 5 minutes at most, or until it reaches 218° F. Stir frequently during these final minutes of cooking and partly cover the pot to prevent spattering.

Off the heat, skim off any foam and remove the slice of ginger. Pour preserves into hot, sterilized jars to within ⅛ inch of the lips. Wipe the rims clean, attach new lids, and screw caps on tightly. Invert the jars briefly to create a quick vacuum seal or process in a boiling water bath, submerged by 1 inch, for 10 minutes

Note: If fresh blackberries are not available in your area in the summer, check the freezer section at your market for dry-packed frozen blackberries. The brands I have tried offer berries in a near-ripe state with a full fresh taste, which is perfect for preserving.

YIELD: 4⅔ cups

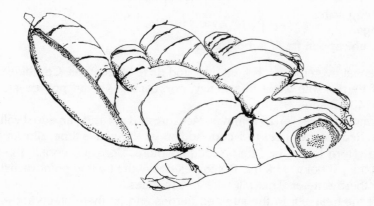

Blueberry Blackberry Preserves

There are just enough dark, woodsy blackberries in this preserve to highlight the blueberry's soft, watery sweetness.

With its low-key sugar and acid balance, Blueberry Blackberry Preserves flatters a wide variety of breads. How about trying it on Banana Bran Muffins or English Muffins with Yogurt (see index)?

5 cups blueberries (1½ pounds)
½ pound fresh or frozen dry-pack blackberries
⅓ cup water
Sugar
½ tablespoon fresh lemon juice

Preheat oven to 350° F. Pick over and rinse blueberries. Combine both types of berries with water in a heavy, nonreactive 4-quart pot, cover, and bake for 40 minutes.

Strain off juices for 15 minutes. Measure and set aside an equal volume of sugar. Reduce the juices to 1 cup. Add sugar ½ cup at a time, allowing the liquid to return to the boil before adding more. Continue cooking until it reaches the jell point, which is 8 degrees above the boiling point measured on your thermometer. This will take 2-4 minutes.

Off the heat, stir in the strained berries and let them steep in the hot juices for 15 minutes.

Return preserves to a boil. Add lemon juice and another ¼ cup sugar. Cook no longer than 10 minutes, until thermometer reads 218° F.

Off the heat, fill hot, sterilized jars to within ⅛ inch of lips. Wipe off the rims, attach new lids, and screw the caps on tightly. Invert jars briefly for a quick vacuum seal or process in a boiling water bath, submerged by 1 inch, for 10 minutes.

YIELD: 3 cups

Red Raspberry Preserves

It's quick, simple, and possibly the most delicious preserve there is. These preserves enhance any breakfast, served on an English Muffin (see index), and can be very dressy for high tea with Cream Scones and Butter Pecan Muffins (see index).

A look through Chapter 9 will show you how many delicious dessert alliances can be made with these preserves. This recipe is the star of the Linzer Torte and the fillip of the Fresh Peach Melba (see index). You can successfully freeze it with cream to make a luscious ice cream or dilute it with simple syrup to make stunning frozen sorbet.

3 pounds red raspberries
Sugar

Preheat the oven to 350° F. Bake berries, covered, in a heavy, nonreactive 4-quart pot for 40 minutes. The berries should render their juices but remain whole.

Strain off raspberry juices for 15 minutes. Measure the juice and warm an equal volume of sugar in a 250° F. oven for 10 minutes. Bring juice to a boil and stir in the warm sugar ½ cup at a time, allowing it to return to the boil before adding more. Cook until the mixture reaches the jell point, which is 8 degrees above the boiling temperature measured on your thermometer. This will take 5-10 minutes.

Skim foam from the jelly and fold in the raspberries. Let them steep in the jelly for 15 minutes. Bring the preserve mixture to the boil again. Add 1 last cup of sugar ½ cup at a time. Continue cooking until it reaches the jell point. This will take 7-10 minutes. Stir frequently during this time to prevent sticking.

Skim preserves and fill hot, sterilized jars to within ⅛ inch of lips. Wipe the rims clean, attach new lids, and screw the caps on tightly. Invert jars briefly for a quick vacuum seal or submerge them by 1 inch in a boiling water bath for 10 minutes.

YIELD: 5 cups

Blueberry Raspberry Preserves

This preserve of blueberries and raspberries is a special midsummer treat to serve with warm muffins or scones (see index for recipes).

2 pounds fresh blueberries
1 pound red raspberries
½ cup water
1 ½ cups sugar
1 tablespoon fresh lemon juice

Preheat the oven to 350° F.

Rinse and pick over the blueberries. Combine both types of berries with water in a heavy, nonreactive 4-quart pot. Bake for 30 minutes, covered, or until berries are floating in liquid.

Strain berries for 20 minutes. Reduce juice if necessary to get 1 ½ cups. Bring juice to a simmer. Add sugar ½ cup at a time along with 1 teaspoon lemon juice. Boil it until it reaches the jell point, which is 8 degrees above the boiling temperature measured on your thermometer. This will take about 5 minutes.

Off the heat, stir in the berries and let them steep in jelly for 15 minutes.

Add remaining lemon juice and return preserves to a boil. Cook on medium for 10 more minutes, stirring frequently. The mixture will thicken, and the thermometer will rise to 212-214° F.

Off the heat, fill hot, sterilized jars to within ⅛ inch of the lips. Wipe the rims clean, attach new lids, and screw the caps on tightly. Invert the jars briefly for a quick seal or process in a boiling water bath for 10 minutes, submerged by 1 inch.

YIELD: about 4 cups

Apple Red Raspberry Preserves

This pair of fruits produces a preserve of tart flavor, floral aroma, and great pectin strength. They cook into a lovely crimson mixture of tiny seeds, soft pulp, and firm apple slices.

Serve this luscious preserve on the Apple Cinnamon Muffins, Grapenuts Muffins, or Cream Scones (see index). It will also perform beautifully as a sauce on French Toast or when frozen in a sorbet.

2 pounds firm, tart apples (Granny Smith, Jonathan, or Cortland)
1½ pounds red raspberries
½ cup water
Sugar

Peel, quarter, core and thinly slice the apples. Combine apple pieces with raspberries and water in a heavy, nonreactive 4-quart saucepan. Bring liquid to a boil, regulate heat to a simmer, cover, and cook for 20 minutes. Check once or twice to stir and make sure the pot is maintaining a gentle simmer.

Strain the hot juices from the fruit pieces for 15 minutes. Measure this volume and set aside an equal volume of sugar.

Bring fruit juice to a boil and add the sugar ½ cup at a time, waiting for the liquids to return to the boil before adding more. Continue boiling to the jell point, which is 8 degrees above the boiling temperature measured on your thermometer. This will take about 5 minutes.

Off the heat, stir fruit pieces into the hot jelly. Let them steep for 15 minutes.

Return the preserves to the boil and cook 5 minutes, stirring quite often to prevent sticking. The mixture will be quite thick, and its temperature will rise to 204° F.

Off the heat, skim off foam and pour preserves into hot, sterilized jars to within ⅛ inch of the lips. Wipe the rims clean, attach new lids, and screw caps on tightly. Invert the jars briefly for a quick vacuum seal or process in a boiling water bath, submerged by 1 inch, for 10 minutes.

YIELD: 5⅓ cups

Peach Preserves with Raspberries

Peaches with red raspberries is a combination made famous by Escoffier's Pêche Melba dessert, a recipe for which I offer a variation in Chapter 9. In fact, this preserve could make a wonderful Philadelphia-Style Ice Cream or soft-frozen sorbet (see index), if you want to play up its dessert potential. But try it first as a spread on Cream Scones or Butter Pecan Muffins (see index). These flavors are wonderful together at room temperature.

9 peaches (2½ pounds)
½ cup water
1 pound red raspberries
Pectin Stock, as needed (see index)
1 tablespoon fresh lemon juice
2½ cups sugar

Immerse the peaches in simmering water for 30 seconds. Dip them in cold water and peel. Halve peaches, remove pits and slice into ½-inch wedges.

Combine peaches with water in a deep, nonreactive 8-quart pot. Bring water to a boil, reduce heat to a simmer, cover, and cook for 15 minutes. Uncover every 5 minutes to stir and check for sticking.

After 15 minutes, add the raspberries and continue cooking gently for another 15 minutes, stirring at regular intervals.

Strain the peach and raspberry juices for 15 minutes. There will be about 2 cups of liquid. If there is substantially more juice, reduce it to 2 cups. In case there is noticeably less, add Pectin Stock (see index) to make 2 cups.

Reheat the strained liquid with the lemon juice and add 2 cups sugar, ½ cup at a time, allowing mixture to return to the boil before adding more. Continue cooking until it reaches the jell point, which is 8 degrees above the boiling temperature measured on your thermometer. This will take about 10 minutes.

Off the heat, skim the jelly and stir in the fruit pieces. Allow them to steep for 15 minutes.

Return the preserves to a boil and add the last ½ cup sugar. Cook for up to 10 minutes or until the temperature reaches 215° F. Take the pot off the heat every 2 minutes to stir. Use a long-handled spoon to mix this thickened mixture, for it will sputter and spit when stirred.

Fill hot, sterilized jars to within ⅛ inch of the lips. Wipe the rims clean, attach new lids, and screw caps on tightly. Invert the jars briefly for a quick seal or process them in a boiling water bath, submerged by 1 inch, for 10 minutes.

YIELD: 4½ cups

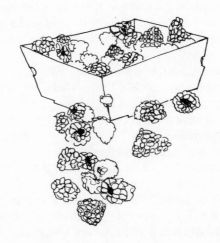

Pear and Grape Preserves

Pears and grapes can be cooked into the sweet preserves that result from this recipe or into a no-sugar jam (see index).

Savor this pear and grape combination on Oatmeal Muffins, Butter Pecan Muffins, or Drop Scones (see index).

3 pounds Concord grapes (3 cups strained juice)
1 cup water
3 pounds ripe Bartlett pears
3 cups sugar

Rinse and stem the grapes. Bring them to a simmer with 1 cup water in a heavy, nonreactive 4-quart pan. Cover the pot and simmer slowly for 30 minutes. Lift the cover regularly to stir and crush the grapes against the side of the pot.

Strain grape juice through a sieve lined with cheesecloth. In an hour you should have about 3 cups juice. If there is less, add water to make up the difference. If there is more, reduce it to 3 cups.

Peel, quarter, and core the pears. Thinly slice the pears and combine in a 4-quart pan with the grape juice. Bring juice to a boil, regulate heat to a gentle simmer, cover, and cook for 10 minutes.

Off the heat, strain the grape juice from the pears for 15 minutes. Reduce this juice to 3 cups.

Bring juice to a boil and add 3 cups sugar ½ cup at a time, allowing the liquid to return to the boil between additions. Continue boiling until it reaches the jell point, which is 8 degrees above the boiling point measured on your thermometer. This will take 5–7 minutes.

Off the heat, stir in the pear pieces and steep for 15 minutes.

Return the preserves to the boil and cook over medium-high heat until it reaches the jell point. This may take as long as 15 minutes. Stir quite frequently to prevent sticking and partly cover the top to contain spatters. Cook preserves a full minute at the jell temperature.

Off the heat, skim the surface and pour preserves into hot, sterilized jars to within ⅛ inch of the lips. Wipe the rims clean, attach new lids, and screw caps on tightly. Invert the jars briefly for a quick vacuum seal or process in a boiling water bath for 10 minutes, submerged by 1 inch.

YIELD: 4½ cups

Apple Grape Preserves

The rich scent of apples and grapes sitting in the warm September sun at roadside stands recalls pleasant memories of fall harvest. Now you can capture this evocative fragrance in a preserve to enjoy through-out the winter.

Apple Grape Preserves taste wonderful served with freshly baked Apple Cinnamon Muffins (see index).

3 pounds Concord grapes (3 cups cooked and strained)
½ cup water
2 cups Granny Smith or Yellow Delicious apples
Sugar

Rinse and remove grapes from their stems. Combine water with grapes in a heavy, nonreactive 4-quart pan and bring liquid to a boil. Reduce the heat to a simmer, cover, and cook 15 minutes.

Strain grape juice for 2 hours or overnight. Reserve 3 cups.

Peel, quarter, and core the apples. Slice them into narrow wedges. Combine the apple pieces with grape juice in a 5-quart pan. Bring juice to the boil, turn down the heat, and simmer gently, uncovered, for 10 minutes. Apples will soften but remain whole.

Strain juice from the apples for 15 minutes. Measure strained juice and set aside an equal volume of sugar. Bring juice to a boil and add sugar ½ cup at a time, allowing juice to return to the boil before adding more. Continue cooking over high heat until the mixture reaches the jell point, which is 8 degrees above the boiling point measured on your thermometer. This will take less than 5 minutes.

Remove the jelly from the heat. Stir in the apple pieces and let them steep and absorb the juice for 15 minutes.

Return the preserves to the boil. Stir in an additional ½ cup of sugar. Let the mixture cook at a boil until it reaches 218° F. When the temperature begins to drop, remove the pot from the heat. Total cooking time for this last step will be at least 5 minutes and no more than 10 minutes. Stir the pot frequently to prevent sticking.

Off the heat, skim foam from the preserves and fill hot, sterilized jars to within ⅛ inch of the lips. Wipe the rims clean, attach new lids, and screw the caps on tightly.

Invert the jars briefly for a quick vacuum seal or process in a boiling water bath, submerged by 1 inch, for 10 minutes.

YIELD: 4 cups.

Four-Berry Preserves

Since blueberries, red raspberries, blackberries, and strawberries are not at peak ripeness at the same time, you will have to plan ahead to make this preserve. Freeze some strawberries and red raspberries and defrost them when you have fresh blueberries and blackberries at hand. This combination is definitely worth the effort.

This preserve is so rich in aroma and flavor that a warm, chewy English Muffin (see index) or any of its variations would be a welcome partner.

1 pound blueberries
1 pound red raspberries
½ pound blackberries
½ pound strawberries
½ cup water
1½ tablespoons fresh lemon juice
2½ cups sugar

Preheat the oven to 350° F. Combine all 4 fruits and water in a heavy, nonreactive 5-quart pot and bake, covered, for 50 minutes. Strain off the juices for 15 minutes.

Reduce the berry juices to 2 cups. Pour in 1 tablespoon lemon juice and return to a boil. Add 2 cups sugar ½ cup at a time, allowing the mixture to return to the boil before adding more. Continue cooking until it reaches the jell point, which is 8 degrees above the boiling temperature measured on your thermometer. This will take 5-7 minutes.

Off the heat, stir fruit pieces into the jelly and let them steep for 15 minutes.

Bring preserves to the boil. Add ½ tablespoon lemon juice and remaining ½ cup sugar. Boil the mixture, stirring frequently, for up to 10 minutes or until it reaches 218° F.

Off the heat, skim off foam and fill hot, sterilized jars to within ⅛ inch of the lips. Wipe the rims clean, attach new lids, and screw caps on tightly. Invert jars briefly for a quick vacuum seal or process in a boiling water bath, submerged by 1 inch, for 10 minutes.

YIELD: 5 cups

Cherry Preserves with Cassis

As in the Cherry and Red Raspberry Jam (see index), here a richly tart partner energizes the cherry flavor, which often fades in the presence of sugar. The concentrated aroma of black currant brandy in this recipe adds a bit of complexity by developing the presence of the currants.

This preserve is delicious on Risen Biscuits, Whole Wheat English Muffins, and Buckwheat Muffins (see index).

**2 pounds red currants (1½ cups strained juice), generally available
    at fruit stands, orchards, and farmers' markets
½ cup water
3 pounds pitted sour cherries
2½ cups sugar
⅓ cup crème de cassis (black currant liqueur)**

Preheat the oven to 350° F. Bake red currants, stems on, in a heavy, nonreactive 4-quart pot with ½ cup water, covered, for 30 minutes. Strain juices for 2 hours or overnight. Reserve 1½ cups juice for this recipe and store the rest for later use.

Place cherries in a 5-quart pot. Heat and stir until the cherries have exuded some juice. Bring the juice to a boil, reduce heat to a simmer, and cook, partly covered, for 15 minutes. Strain the cherry juices for 20 minutes. Reduce cherry juice to 1 cup.

Add the red currant juice and bring liquid to a boil. Add 2 cups sugar ½ cup at a time, allowing the mixture to return to the boil before adding more. Continue cooking until it reaches the jell point, which is 8 degrees above the boiling temperature measured on your thermometer. This will take 5–7 minutes.

Off the heat, stir the cherry pieces into the hot jelly and steep for 15 minutes.

Return preserves to a boil and add the remaining ½ cup sugar. Continue cooking until the temperature reaches the jell point. This will take about 5 minutes.

Pour in the crème de cassis and cook preserves 2 minutes more.

Off the heat, fill hot, sterilized jars to within ⅛ inch of lips. Wipe the rims clean, attach new lids, and screw caps on tightly. Invert jars briefly for a quick vacuum seal or process in a boiling water bath, submerged by 1 inch, for 10 minutes.

YIELD: 4 cups

Strawberry Blackberry Preserves

Why not save a jar of this preserve of succulent summer strawberries and blackberries for a late fall brunch buffet? Surround it with steamy fresh Buckwheat Muffins and textured Grapenuts Muffins (see index).

2 pounds strawberries, 25 percent only partly ripened
1 pound fresh or frozen dry-pack blackberries
⅓ cup water
Apple Pectin Stock (if needed) (see index)
1 tablespoon fresh lemon juice
2½ cups sugar

Preheat oven to 350° F.

Rinse strawberries, hull, and cut larger ones in half so they are all of uniform size. Combine them with blackberries and water in a heavy, nonreactive 5-quart pot. Cover and bake for 40 minutes.

Strain the berry juices for 20 minutes. If there is less than 2 cups, add Apple Pectin Stock to make 2 cups. If there is more than 2 cups, reduce juices rapidly to that amount. Stir in 2 teaspoons lemon juice.

Bring juices to a boil and add 2 cups sugar ½ cup at a time, allowing the liquid to return to the boil before adding more. Continue boiling until it reaches the jell point, which is 8 degrees above the jell temperature measured on your thermometer. This will take up to 10 minutes.

Off the heat, skim off the foam. Pour in the berries and let steep for 15 minutes. Return preserves to a boil. Add the remaining ½ cup sugar and 1 teaspoon lemon juice. Cook until temperature reaches 218° F., as long as 10 minutes.

Off the heat, skim off foam and fill hot, sterilized jars to within ⅛ inch of lips. Wipe the rims clean, attach new lids, and screw caps on tightly. Invert the jars briefly for a quick vacuum seal or process 10 minutes in a boiling water bath, covered by 1 inch.

YIELD: 4 cups

Strawberry Preserves

What could be more gratifying than a thick layer of dark, sweet strawberry preserves on a warm English Muffin or Cream Scone (see index)? In fact, Strawberry Preserves complements all breads and doubles as a tasty sauce on fruit and ice cream.

3 pounds strawberries, 25 percent only partly ripened
1 cup Pectin Stock (see index)
4 teaspoons lemon juice
2½ cups sugar

Rinse and hull the strawberries. Cut larger ones into pieces so all are of uniform size. Place berries in a heavy, nonreactive 5-quart pan. Heat and stir them over medium heat as they warm and render their juices. Turn the berries over with a spoon every minute or so, so they are all exposed to the bottom of the pan. Cook until they all soften and exude juice but still maintain their shape, about 10-15 minutes.

Strain off the juices for 15 minutes. Reduce these over high heat to 1 cup. Add the Pectin Stock and 1 tablespoon lemon juice and return liquid to the boil. Stir in 2 cups sugar ½ cup at a time, allowing juices to return to a boil before adding more. Continue cooking until it reaches the jell point, which is 8 degrees above the boiling temperature measured on your thermometer. This will happen within 5 minutes.

Off the heat, skim foam from the surface and stir the berries into the hot jelly. Let them steep in the jelly for 15 minutes.

Return the preserves to a boil and stir in the remaining teaspoon of lemon juice and the remaining ½ cup sugar. Cook the preserves, watching the thermometer carefully. It will rise to 216°F. or so in 5 minutes. Stir it frequently and partly cover with the lid when it starts to spatter. The minute the temperature begins to fall after the first 5 minutes, take the pot off the heat. Do not cook it longer than 10 minutes.

Skim the surface again and fill hot, sterilized jars to within ⅛ inch of the lips. Wipe the rims clean, attach new lids, and screw caps on tightly. Invert jars briefly for a quick vacuum seal or process in a boiling water bath for 10 minutes, submerged by 1 inch.

YIELD: 3½ cups

Spicy Blueberry Preserves

Fresh, plump blueberries are so easy to eat out of hand or pop into muffin batter that their flavor potential is rarely developed beyond this point. But they can be rich, tart, and more intensely delicious when cooked in a preserve. The addition of spices further heightens the drama of their concentrated flavor.

This preserve is wonderful with warm Butter Pecan Muffins, Buckwheat Muffins, and Drop Scones (see index). It also serves as a beautiful and tasty garnish in Blueberry Pecan Cheesecake (see index). You will find it equally delicious when frozen in ice cream and sorbet or warmed in a sauce for baked stuffed peaches (see index).

3 pounds blueberries
1 4-inch cinnamon stick
Bouquet garni: **3 each: 2-inch strips fresh lemon peel, whole**
    cloves, and allspice berries
½ cup Pectin Stock (see index)
1 tablespoon fresh lemon juice
2½ cups sugar

Preheat the oven to 350° F. Pick over and rinse berries. Bake berries in a heavy, nonreactive 4-quart pot, covered, for 30 minutes.

Strain the berries for 15 minutes. Tie lemon peel and spices in cheesecloth with cotton twine and submerge in the juices. Reduce to 1½ cups. Add Pectin Stock and lemon juice. Return juice to the boil and add 2 cups sugar ½ cup at a time, allowing the mixture to return to the boil before adding more. Continue cooking until it reaches the jell point, which is 8 degrees above the boiling temperature measured on your thermometer. This will take 5-10 minutes.

Off the heat, stir in the berries and let them steep for 15 minutes. Bring preserves to a boil. Add remaining ½ cup sugar and continue cooking, stirring frequently and covering pot as needed to prevent spattering, for 10 minutes or until a thermometer reads 210° F.

Off the heat, and remove the *bouquet garni*. Fill hot, sterilized jars to within ⅛ inch of the lips. Wipe the rims clean, attach new lids, and screw the caps on tightly. Invert the jars briefly for a quick vacuum seal or process in a boiling water bath for 10 minutes, submerged by 1 inch.

YIELD: 4½ cups

Tropical Pineapple Preserves

The idea of pairing fragrant vanilla with the sweet acidic pineapple was one of my happiest preserving inspirations, though it was based on geography rather than taste. When I learned that pineapple is native to Guadeloupe in the West Indies I knew there had to be some promise in combining it with vanilla, whose home is nearby Mexico.

This aromatic preserve, full of small fruit nuggets, is delicious on Tea Brack, Cream Scones, or English Muffins (see index).

2 pounds peeled, quartered, and cored fresh pineapple
½ cup water
1 cup Pectin Stock (see index)
2½ cups sugar
½ tablespoon lemon juice
½ tablespoon vanilla extract (preferably Mexican)

Cut the pineapple quarters into 6 lengthwise slices. Cut across these at ¼-inch intervals to make thin wedges. (If you prefer to use a food processor, cut pineapple quarters into 8 pieces and chop 2 quarters at a time with rapid on-and-off motions until pieces are no bigger than ½-inch bits.) Combine the pineapple pieces with water in a heavy, nonreactive 5-quart pot and bring to a boil. Lower the heat to a simmer, cover, and simmer the pineapple for 15 minutes, lifting the lid to stir every 5 minutes.

Strain off the pineapple juice for 15 minutes. Reduce juices to 1 cup and add 1 cup Pectin Stock.

Bring liquid to a boil and add 2 cups sugar ½ cup at a time, allowing the mixture to return to the boil before adding more. Continue boiling until the mixture reaches the jell point, which is 8 degrees above the boiling temperature measured on your thermometer. This will happen within 2 minutes. Maintain the boil for a full minute after reaching the jell point.

(Recipe continues on following page.)

Off the heat, stir the pineapple pulp into the hot jelly to steep for 15 minutes.

Stir in lemon juice and return preserves to a boil. Add the last ½ cup sugar and cook on medium for 10 minutes, stirring frequently as liquid reduces. When the preserve begins to sputter and spit, partially cover the pot with a lid while continuing to stir and watch the temperature at 2-minute intervals. The temperature will rise as high as 216° F.

Off the heat, let preserves cool for 5 minutes in the pan before stirring in the vanilla. Fill hot, sterilized jars to within ⅛ inch of the lips. Wipe the rims clean, attach new lids, and screw caps on tightly. Invert jars briefly for a quick vacuum seal or process in a boiling water bath for 10 minutes, submerged by 1 inch.

YIELD: 3½ cups

Pineapple Lemon Preserves

This is a beautiful golden preserve full of engaging pineapple strands. Lemon juice balances the sugar and emphasizes the pineapple's acidic sweetness.

Try this preserve with Risen Biscuits, Banana Bran Muffins, or Cream Scones (see index). It would also make a great topping for cheesecake (see index), substituting a vanilla wafer crust for the pecan sandies and nuts.

2 pounds peeled, quartered, and cored fresh pineapple
Zest of 2 lemons
½ cup water
1½ cups Pectin Stock (see index)
2 tablespoons fresh lemon juice
2¼ cups sugar

Cut the pineapple quarters into 6 lengthwise slices. Cut across these at ¼-inch intervals to make thin wedges. (If you prefer to use a processor, cut pineapple quarters into 8 pieces and chop 2 quarters at a time with rapid on-and-off motions to make ½-inch bits.) Use a vegetable peeler (illustrated in Chapter 2) to pare thin strips of zest from the lemon. Use a sharp paring knife to cut it into thin julienne strips. Combine fruit, lemon zest, and water in a heavy, nonreactive 5-quart pan. Bring liquid to a boil, reduce heat to a simmer, cover, and cook for 20 minutes, stirring regularly.

Strain the pineapple for 15 minutes. Reduce the strained juices to ½ cup. Pour the Pectin Stock and 1 tablespoon lemon juice into the reduced juices and bring to a boil. Stir in 2 cups of the sugar ½ cup at a time, allowing the liquid to return to the boil before adding more. Continue cooking on high heat until the mixture reaches the jell point, which is 8 degrees above the boiling temperature measured on your thermometer. This will happen within 2 minutes. Maintain the boil for a full minute after reaching the jell point.

Off the heat, stir in the pineapple pieces and let them steep in the jelly for 15 minutes. Bring the preserves to the boil, add the remaining table-spoon of lemon juice and the final ¼ cup sugar, and cook to the jell temperature again. This will take about 5 minutes. Maintain the boil again for a full minute after reaching the jell point.

Off the heat, skim foam from the surface and pour preserves into hot, sterilized jars to within ⅛ inch of lips. Wipe the rims clean, attach new lids, and screw caps on tightly. Invert jars briefly for a quick vacuum seal or process in a boiling water bath, submerged by 1 inch, for 10 minutes.

YIELD: 3⅔ cups

Pear Preserves with Pernod

Pernod is a French aperitif scented with aniseed. It imbues the sweet, delicate pear with an exotic aroma much like licorice but softer. The liqueur is added after the preserve is taken off the heat so it will be hot enough to make the alcohol volatile without driving off the fragrant oil.

Buttermilk Currant Scones or Risen Biscuits (see index), hot from the oven, taste delicious with this preserve.

3 pounds Bartlett pears
1 cup water
5 teaspoons fresh lemon juice
1 cup Pectin Stock (see index)
2 cups sugar
½ tablespoon Pernod

Peel and quarter the pears. Trim off cores and stems and cut each quarter into 3 lengthwise slices. Combine pear pieces with water and 1 tablespoon lemon juice in a heavy, nonreactive 4-quart pot. Bring water to a boil, reduce heat to a simmer, cover, and cook for 20 minutes. Lift the lid to stir and check for a gentle simmer every 5 minutes.

Strain off the juices for 15 minutes. Reduce pear juices to 1 cup and combine with 1 cup Pectin Stock.

Bring liquid to a boil. Add sugar ½ cup at a time, allowing the mixture to return to the boil before adding more. Stir in 1 teaspoon lemon juice. Continue to cook until it reaches the jell point, which is 8 degrees above the boiling point measured on your thermometer. This will take about 5 minutes.

Stir the pear pieces into the hot jelly and steep for 15 minutes. Return the preserves to the boil. Add 1 teaspoon lemon juice and cook until the preserves return to the jell point. This may take up to 10 minutes.

Off the heat, skim off any foam and stir in the Pernod. Pour into hot, sterilized jars to within ⅛ inch of lips. Wipe the rims clean, attach new lids, and screw caps on tightly. Invert jars briefly for a quick vacuum seal or process in a boiling water bath, submerged by 1 inch, for 10 minutes.

YIELD: 3⅔ cups

Three-Onion Preserves

Who said it couldn't be done? Onions make a wonderful and unusual preserve cooked with Apple Pectin Stock. As it cooks, tender onion rings form an appealing web of circles firmly suspended in a lovely amber jelly. The preserve tastes fully of onions with a mild jelly finish, qualities flattering to both breads and cold meats.

Try this preserve on the Oatmeal, Buckwheat, or Cornmeal Muffins as well as the Whole Wheat English Muffins (see index). It is also delicious served with cold roast pork, smoked ham, and roast beef.

1 ½ pounds onions
3 ½ cups Apple Pectin Stock (see index)
1 ½ tablespoons fresh lemon juice
Sugar

Peel the onions and trim off the root ends. Thinly slice them and place in a heavy, nonreactive 5-quart pot with the Apple Pectin Stock. (If you are using a food processor, use the thin slicing disc for this job.) Bring liquid to a boil. Reduce the heat to a simmer and cook, uncovered, for 15 minutes.

Strain the stock from the onion slices for 15 minutes. Measure the stock and set aside an equal volume of sugar. Return the liquid to a boil, stir in the lemon juice, and begin adding the sugar ½ cup at a time. Allow the stock to return to the boil before adding more sugar.

After all the sugar is added, let the jelly boil until it reaches the jell point, which is 8 degrees above the boiling point measured on your thermometer. This will take 7-10 minutes. Boil jelly a full minute at the jell point.

Stir the onion pieces into the hot jelly and let them steep for 15 minutes.

Return the preserves to the boil and cook on medium-high for 10-12 minutes, that is, until the jell point is reached. Take it from the heat even if it has not jelled in 12 minutes. Check its volume and reduce, if necessary, to 1 quart.

Off the heat, skim any foam from the surface and ladle preserves into hot, sterilized jars to within ⅛ inch of the lip. Wipe the rims clean, attach new lids, and screw caps on tightly.

Invert the jars briefly for a quick vacuum seal or process in a boiling water bath, submerged by 1 inch, for 10 minutes.

YIELD: 4 cups

8

BREADS AND MUFFINS

As much as I love homemade fruit preserves, I wouldn't sit down and casually eat a jarful at one sitting. How could those elegant Florentine youths of Boccaccio's day spoon rich preserves directly onto their pampered palates? Why did 17th-century English hostesses serve molded jellies for dessert? So much of such a good thing must have been positively palate-numbing!

I am much more intrigued by the combined pleasures of a rich preserve and a slice of bread. The first bite yields only the bread's firm texture and a faint scent of yeast. Then suddenly the tongue's sweet and sour receptors are flooded with the rich concentration of fruit. The characteristic aroma of the preserve comes on strong, while the soft intricate texture of the fruit pieces blends with the toothsome bread. To my mind, the happiest marriage is made.

Bread is the quiet partner that extends our awareness of the taste of homemade preserves. Think of the sensuous moments in store as you consume rich Strawberry Preserves on a fresh, warm English Muffin (see index). The yeasty aroma will linger as a natural foil for the sugar and acid in fruits. Or consider the flattery accorded jam or marmalade by the fragrant grains in Grapenut Muffins or Buckwheat Muffins (see index).

All the breads, muffins, biscuits, and griddle cakes in this chapter share features attractive to those of us whose interest is primarily in preserves. First, they are so easy that a novice baker can succeed with them. You won't need a great deal of time or an electric appliance to assemble them. The recipes for yeast-risen English Muffins, Risen Biscuits, and Buckwheat Blinis (see index) do require a minimal rising time of 1-2 hours. But only the Tea Brack recipe (see index) requires you to plan far enough in advance to steep the raisins overnight in tea.

I have chosen breads that offer a wide range of surfaces, from the tender, flaky Cream Scones to the firm, chewy English Muffins and the crispy Giant Sunday Popover (see index). They satisfy the need to experience a textured fullness in the mouth without detracting from the preserves.

Bread flavors were a consideration, too. I did not select any sweet breads. Most recipes play on the scent of the grains, the unctuous warmth of butter, or, at most, the aroma of a nut, as in Butter Pecan Muffins (see index). These breads are not intended to compete with the flavors in the jams. You will find sour ingredients, as in the English Muffins with Yogurt (see index), and occasionally a bitter element like cold tea in the Tea Brack (see index). These contrasting tastes are intended to draw attention to the sweet fruit character of preserves.

If you do not have time for baking or are planning a party beyond your baking capacity, muffins, croissants, or sandwich loaves purchased from the local baker will be most satisfying substitutes to serve with your homemade jams and jellies. Sometimes, in fact, a store-bought cracker makes the perfect complement. One of my favorite snacks is a spoonful of seethingly hot Jalapeño Pepper Jelly (see index) over a thick layer of cream cheese on a crisp English water biscuit.

Heat breads before serving them so they warm your preserves and expand the scent of fruit with the aroma of fresh bread.

BASIC BAKING TECHNIQUES

A few basic rules apply to all these bread recipes despite their technical differences.

- Unless otherwise specified in the recipe, begin with all ingredients at room temperature.
- Measure dry ingredients in metal cups using a clean dip-and-sweep motion.
- Measure liquids in heatproof glass measuring cups.

- Place a mercury oven thermometer in your oven to verify its temperature before baking. Ovens change calibrated settings surprisingly quickly and need to be checked with a thermometer each time you bake (simply leave it in the oven) or recalibrated every few months.

Ingredients

Large eggs and unsalted butter are standard ingredients in all these recipes.

The recipes call for several kinds of grain flours, including buckwheat, cornmeal, and oatmeal, as well as wheat flours of various gluten strengths, from the highly elastic bread flour to the softer, low-gluten cake flour. Buy fresh flours if your supplies have been stored for more than 2 months at room temperature or more than 6 months refrigerated or frozen.

The techniques for assembling ingredients are designed either to inhibit or to expand the gluten strength in the wheat flour and, in this way, influence the texture of the bread. In the baking powder bread recipes, which include the muffins, zucchini bread, tea brack, popover, and scones, the flour is gently worked into the wet ingredients. The dough or batter is stirred until the ingredients are just blended. Additional mixing will only tighten the flour's gluten muscle. If any of your baking powder breads rise to a jutting peak rather than a soft mound shape, you will know that the batter was overbeaten.

In the yeast breads, by contrast, you definitely want to promote gluten activity by pulling and stretching the dough. This kneading activity gives the English Muffins and Risen Biscuits (see index) a firm, chewy texture. However, the yeast in the Russian Buckwheat Blinis with Blackberry Sauce recipe (see index) is used only to flavor the dough so no kneading activity is called for.

Butter Pecan Muffins

Usually all one needs to enjoy the rich flavor of steamy, warm pecan muffins is the muffin itself. But by the time a second muffin is on your plate, so is a mild Orange Marmalade and a tablespoon of Spicy Blueberry Preserves (see index). In this case, more is better.

6 tablespoons unsalted butter
½ cup chopped pecans
3 tablespoons brown sugar
4 teaspoons baking powder
2 cups unbleached flour
½ teaspoon salt
1 cup milk
2 large eggs

Preheat the oven to 350° F. Butter a pan that holds 12 muffins.

Melt 6 tablespoons butter and reserve it. Toast the pecan pieces for 10 minutes in the oven. Raise the temperature setting to 400° F.

Measure the sugar, baking powder, flour, and salt into a 2-quart bowl and stir well. Make a well in the center and pour in the milk and eggs. Beat the eggs with the milk and gradually incorporate the dry ingredients. Stir together until just blended.

Fold the melted butter and warm pecans into this batter. Ladle it into the molds and bake for 15 minutes, until the muffins are puffed and lightly browned. Let them cool in the pan for 5 minutes. Unmold and serve warm with jam or preserves.

YIELD: 12 muffins

Cornmeal Muffins

Here is a muffin recipe that can be modified for almost any occasion. Made as printed below, it can be served at a meal or tea with the delicate Lime Marmalade or Peach and Blueberry Jam (see index). If you were to substitute brown sugar for white, bacon drippings for butter, a coarsely ground cornmeal, and buttermilk for milk, you would have a Country-Style Cornmeal Muffin (see below). This would call for a jar of zesty Apricot Orange Jam or Damson Plum Jam (see index).

2 tablespoons sugar
3 tablespoons unsalted butter at room temperature
¾ cup cornmeal
3 large eggs
1 cup milk
1 cup unbleached flour
1 tablespoon baking powder
½ teaspoon salt
¼ teaspoon freshly ground black pepper

Preheat the oven to 400° F. Butter a pan that holds 12 muffins.

Cream sugar with butter in a 2-quart bowl. Stir in the cornmeal, the eggs, 1 at a time, and the milk.

Measure flour, baking powder, salt, and pepper into a 1-quart bowl and mix well. Pour the dry mixture over the wet one and stir together until just blended.

Ladle the batter into the molds and bake for 20 minutes until the muffins are puffed and golden. Let them cool in the pan for 5 minutes. Unmold and serve them warm with jam or preserves.

YIELD: 12 muffins

Country-Style Cornmeal Muffins

This is a variation of Cornmeal Muffins.

2 tablespoons brown sugar
3 tablespoons bacon drippings
¾ cup coarse cornmeal
3 large eggs
1 cup buttermilk
1 cup unbleached white flour
1 tablespoon baking powder
½ teaspoon salt
¼ teaspoon freshly ground black pepper

Follow the directions for the Cornmeal Muffins.

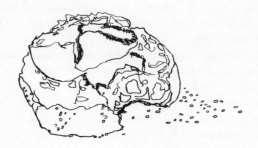

Oatmeal Muffins

Sometimes you want a bread to showcase your preserving prowess. An oatmeal muffin offers just the right profile, with its slightly chewy texture and warm, fresh grain scent. Now is your chance to serve that fabulous Double Black Raspberry Jam or the exotic Kiwifruit Mint Jam (see index) and really wow your guests.

1 cup instant oatmeal
1 cup milk
2 tablespoons unsalted butter
3 tablespoons brown sugar
1½ cups unbleached flour
4 teaspoons baking powder
½ teaspoon salt
2 large eggs

Preheat the oven to 400° F. Butter a pan that holds 12 muffins.

Measure the oatmeal into a 2-quart bowl. Heat the milk and butter to a simmer. Pour this hot mixture over the oatmeal and let it stand for 10 minutes.

Measure and mix together the sugar, flour, baking powder, and salt in a 1-quart bowl.

Beat the eggs into the oatmeal mixture. Pour the dry mixture over the wet one and stir together until just blended.

Ladle the batter into the molds and bake for 15 minutes, until the muffins are puffed and browned. Let them cool in the pan for 5 minutes. Unmold and eat warm with jam or marmalade.

YIELD: 12 muffins

Apple Cinnamon Muffins

This muffin can easily become the delicious by-product of a Pectin Stock recipe. Simply press the strained apple pieces through a food mill and fold the applesauce into the other muffin ingredients. The soft apple pulp gives the bread a moist, delicate texture and cinnamon revives the apple's floral scent. One of the snappy no-sugar jams would taste good with this subtle muffin. My choice would be the No-Sugar Blackberry Jam or No-Sugar Pear and Blueberry Jam (see index).

3 tablespoons soft unsalted butter
2 tablespoons brown sugar
3 large eggs
1 cup unsweetened applesauce
1½ cups unbleached flour
½ teaspoon ground cinnamon
½ teaspoon salt
4 teaspoons baking powder

Preheat the oven to 400° F. Butter a pan that holds 12 muffins.

Cream 3 tablespoons butter with brown sugar in a 2-quart bowl. Add eggs 1 at a time, mixing each in well. Stir in the applesauce.

Measure the flour, cinnamon, salt, and baking powder into a 1-quart bowl and stir together. Pour dry mixture over the wet one and stir together until they are just blended.

Ladle the batter into the molds and bake for 15 minutes, until muffins are puffed and browned. Let them cool in the pan for 5 minutes. Unmold and serve them warm with butter and marmalade.

YIELD: 12 muffins

Buckwheat Muffins

Watch this muffin cause eyebrows to rise in delight at its gutsy array of scents and flavors. The buckwheat flour has a bitter tang; the buttermilk is pleasingly sour. Even the lard and molasses that shorten and sweeten this bread have distinct personalities. Serve an assertive fruit flavor that can hold its own with this robust partner: Plum Jam with Cardamom, Orange Cranberry Marmalade, Pineapple Lemon Preserves (see index).

3 tablespoons lard
3 tablespoons molasses
½ cup buckwheat flour
1 cup buttermilk
2 large eggs
1 cup unbleached flour
5 teaspoons baking powder
½ teaspoon salt

Preheat the oven to 400° F. Butter a pan that holds 12 muffins.

Cream the lard with the molasses in a 2-quart bowl. Stir in the buckwheat flour and half the buttermilk to make a smooth batter. Beat in the remaining buttermilk and the eggs, 1 at a time.

Measure the unbleached flour, baking powder, and salt into a 1-quart bowl and mix well. Pour the dry mixture over the wet one and stir together until just blended.

Ladle the batter into the molds and bake for 15 minutes, until the muffins are puffed and browned. Let them cool in the pan for 5 minutes. Unmold and serve them warm with butter and jam.

YIELD: 12 muffins

Grapenuts Muffins

In this recipe the rich wheat and malted barley aroma of Grapenuts is magnified by cooking, and its famous gravel-crunch texture is softened to flavorful rubble. Try this muffin with the delicate, quick Blueberry Jam with Mint or the sweet-hot Apple Ginger Jam (see index).

1 cup Grapenuts cereal
1 cup buttermilk
4 tablespoons unsalted butter, melted
3 eggs, lightly beaten
1 cup unbleached flour
4 teaspoons baking powder
2 tablespoons sugar
½ teaspoon salt

Preheat the oven to 400° F. Butter a pan that holds 12 muffins.

Combine Grapenuts, buttermilk, melted butter, and eggs in a 2-quart bowl, stir, and let stand 10 minutes.

Measure flour, baking powder, sugar, and salt into a 1-quart bowl and stir well.

Pour dry mixture over the wet one and stir together until just blended.

Ladle the batter into the molds and bake for 15 minutes, until muffins are puffed and lightly browned. Let them cool in the pan for 5 minutes. Unmold and serve warm with sweet butter and jam.

YIELD: 12 muffins

Banana Bran Muffins

This muffin pairs soft, sweet bananas with the textured whole-grain flavors of wheat and bran. A colorful, acidic preserve such as Kiwifruit Pineapple Jam or Nectarine Orange Jam (see index) would make a tasty partner. You could also serve it with a zucchini or pepper marmalade and enjoy the composition of a vegetable preserve on dark bread.

¼ cup brown sugar
4 tablespoons unsalted butter at room temperature
3 large eggs
2 large bananas, puréed (1 cup)
¾ cup bran
1½ cups whole wheat flour
½ teaspoon salt
4 teaspoons baking powder

Preheat the oven to 400° F. Butter a pan that holds 12 muffins.

Cream brown sugar and butter in a 2-quart bowl. Stir in eggs 1 at a time and add banana purée.

Measure and mix together the bran, flour, salt, and baking powder in a 1-quart bowl. Pour the dry mixture over the wet one and stir until just blended.

Ladle the batter into the molds and bake for 15 minutes, until the muffins are puffed and brown. Let them cool in the pan for 5 minutes. Unmold and eat warm with jam or marmalade.

YIELD: 12 muffins

Zucchini Bread

This is one of my favorite summer breads. I never tire of making substitutions and variations in the recipe. But I always serve it the same way. Slices are cut thin. One side is slathered with fresh cream cheese, the other with Red Currant Jelly or an equally tangy Cherry and Red Raspberry Jam (see index). The sandwiches are cut diagonally into triangles and served with a cup of hot tea.

> 2 cups grated zucchini
> 2 cups whole wheat flour
> 1 cup unbleached white flour
> 1 cup sugar
> 1 teaspoon salt
> 1 teaspoon baking powder
> 1 teaspoon baking soda
> ¼ teaspoon each: mace, cinnamon, ginger, cardamom
> 3 large eggs
> 1 cup salad oil
> 2 teaspoons vanilla
> Grated peel of 1 lemon (optional)
> 1 cup of currants, chopped dried apricots and dates, or chopped
>   nuts (optional)

Preheat the oven to 325° F. Lightly oil a 9-by-5-inch loaf pan or one that has 18 muffin molds.

Grate the zucchini and reserve. Combine flours, sugar, salt, baking powder, soda, and spices in a 2-quart bowl and stir to mix well. Add the eggs to the oil in a 2-cup measure and beat lightly. Stir in the vanilla.

Make a well in the center of the dry ingredients, pour in the wet ones, and stir from the center, slowly incorporating the dry into the wet ingredients. Mix only until a batter forms.

Fold in the zucchini along with optional lemon peel, dried fruits, or nuts and ladle the mixture into the pan or muffin molds. Bake for 1 hour or until a cake tester comes out dry. Allow the bread to cool for 10 minutes in the pan (5 minutes for the muffins) before unmolding. Serve bread at room temperature (serve muffins warm) with an invigorating sweet-tart jelly.

YIELD: 1 large loaf or 18 muffins

Tea Brack

This recipe first intrigued me because tea was an ingredient. I was delighted to find that the tea offered a slightly astringent counterpoint to the otherwise predominately sweet ingredients. My Tea Brack also has an attractively firm texture dotted with chewy sweet bits and crunchy nuts. I prefer to serve it with a lively sweet-sour jelly such as the Grape, Cinnamon Cranberry Apple, or Kir Cocktail Jelly (see index).

¾ **cup white raisins**
¾ **cup dried currants**
1¼ **cups light brown sugar, firmly packed**
1½ **cups cold black tea**
2 **cups unbleached white flour**
1½ **teaspoons baking powder**
½ **teaspoon each: cinnamon and nutmeg**
¼ **teaspoon salt**
½ **cup crushed walnuts**
1 **large egg**
¼ **cup salad oil**

Combine raisins, currants, sugar, and tea in a mixing bowl. Cover and let stand overnight.

Preheat the oven to 325° F. and generously oil a 9-by-5-inch loaf pan.

Blend flour, baking powder, spices, and salt in a large bowl. Crush the walnut pieces to the size of peas and toss them into the dry ingredients.

Make a well in the dry mixture. Add the beaten egg and oil along with the fruit and tea combination. Stir from the center, gradually adding the dry to the wet ingredients to make a smooth batter.

Pour it into the prepared pan and bake for 1½ hours or until a cake tester comes out dry.

Let the loaf cool in the pan for 30 minutes. Loosen the sides and invert to release the bread. Cool to room temperature before serving.

YIELD: 1 large loaf, about 2 dozen slices

Cream Scones

This recipe produces a butter-fragrant and tender biscuit. Dress it with a truly fancy topping like Red Raspberry Jam (see index). The preserves with liqueurs, Nectarine Slices with Grand Marnier, and Pear Preserves with Pernod (see index) are also good here.

2½ cups cake flour
¼ cup sugar
4 teaspoons baking powder
1 teaspoon salt
6 tablespoons cold unsalted butter
⅔ cup light cream
1 egg beaten with 1 tablespoon cream

Preheat the oven to 375°F. Butter and flour a large baking sheet.

Combine flour, sugar, baking powder, and salt in a 2-quart bowl and stir to mix.

Cut the cold butter into 24 small pieces (quarter it lengthwise and cut each quarter crosswise into 6 pieces) and work into the dry ingredients with fingertips or a pastry blender until the texture is mealy. Stir in cream until a ball forms. (It will take 6-8 rapid on-and-off motions to pulverize the butter in the workbowl of a food processor. Add the cream and run the machine until a ball is barely formed.)

Roll the dough out onto a lightly floured work surface. Cut into 2½-inch biscuits with a cutter or the lip of a glass.

Brush tops lightly with egg wash and bake for 15 minutes until the scones are puffed and lightly browned. Cool them briefly, serve warm with jam or marmalade and Crème Fraîche (see index).

YIELD: 16 scones

Scone Variations

Buttermilk Currant Scones

Substitute for light cream:
   ¼ **teaspoon baking soda**
   ⅔ **cup buttermilk**
Add: ½ **cup currants**

Follow directions for Cream Scones, above, with these modifications:
Stir soda into buttermilk after butter is blended into dry ingredients.
When buttermilk begins to foam, stir liquid into the dry ingredients to make
a soft dough.

Fold in the currants on a lightly floured work surface, working the
dough as little as possible.

Proceed to roll out, cut, glaze, and bake the scones as indicated in the
master recipe.

YIELD: 18 2-inch scones

Drop Scones

*The first scones were probably made as these are, dropped onto a
hot griddle and baked quickly. They taste best split and eaten quite
warm with butter and an intense flavor such as Apricot Orange Jam or
Rhubarb Blackberry Jam (see index).*

2 large eggs
5 tablespoons sugar
½ **cup light cream**
1½ **cups cake flour**
1 teaspoon baking powder

Preheat a griddle or heavy 12-inch skillet.

Beat the eggs and sugar together. Stir in the cream. Sift on the flour ½
cup at a time, adding the baking powder to the last addition and mixing each
in thoroughly. (The scones will be the consistency of a thick pancake batter.)

Drop scones onto the hot surface with a serving spoon (2 tablespoons)
and brown on both sides for 5-6 minutes of total cooking time.

Serve hot immediately and pass marmalade and Crème Fraîche (see
index).

YIELD: 12 scones

Giant Sunday Popover

This giant popover is easy to assemble so you'll have time to pour the juice, fry some bacon, and start the Sunday paper while you wait. Its transformation from batter to a puffed and rippled, crispy brown pastry trailing the scent of vanilla will awaken an appetite in even the groggiest diner.

2 tablespoons salad oil
4 tablespoons unsalted butter
3 large eggs
¾ cup milk
¼ teaspoon vanilla extract
¼ teaspoon salt
½ tablespoon sugar
¾ cup unbleached flour, sifted before measuring
¼ teaspoon ground cinnamon
⅛ teaspoon ground ginger
¼ cup Vanilla Sugar (see index)
1 cup fruit sauce made with Cranberry Orange Marmalade or Apple
Red Raspberry Preserves (see index)

Preheat the oven to 425° F. Combine oil and butter in an ovenproof 12-inch skillet. Put the skillet in the hot oven until butter begins to brown, 3–4 minutes.

Lightly beat the eggs with a whisk in a 2-quart bowl. Pour in the milk, vanilla, salt, and sugar, continuing to whisk gently. Sift the flour into a small bowl. Measure it ¼ cup at a time back into the sifter and onto the eggs and milk, whisking until each addition is just blended, though there may be small bits of unincorporated flour. Add the cinnamon and ginger to the last ¼ cup of flour.

Pour the batter into the hot skillet and bake for 25 minutes. The popover will be puffed and brown.

Dust the top with Vanilla Sugar and serve immediately in generous wedges. Pass warm fruit sauce at the table.

YIELD: 6 servings

Russian Buckwheat Blinis with Blackberry Sauce

This is a fitting breakfast for those who rise early to spend a day roving in the country or working in the yard. The ingredients have a wild, wayside appeal. The buckwheat blinis are griddlecakes with a yeasty and slightly bitter taste. The blackberries retain their woodsy floral scent and some acidity even when sweetened. Together they refresh and invigorate an awakening palate.

Blinis

1 package active dry yeast
½ cup lukewarm water
½ cup each: unbleached white flour and buckwheat flour
½ teaspoon salt
½ cup milk
2 large eggs, separated
1 stick (4 ounces) unsalted butter, melted

Blackberry Sauce

1 Master Recipe for Fruit Sauce Made with Jams and Preserves
    (see index)

Garnish

½ cup sour cream

Blinis

Dissolve the yeast in the water. Combine flours with salt in a 2-quart mixing bowl and make a well in the center. Pour in milk, egg yolks, and yeast mixture. Stir wet into dry ingredients to make a smooth batter.

Cover the bowl with plastic wrap and let rise for 2 hours at room temperature or refrigerate overnight.

(Recipe continues on following page.)

If chilled, allow the risen batter to warm for an hour at room temperature. Also warm whites to room temperature.

Heat a 12-inch skillet or griddle and coat it lightly with some butter. Beat egg whites to soft peaks. Spoon 2 tablespoons melted butter and one-third of whites onto the buckwheat batter and stir in gently. Fold in the remaining whites and butter in 2 parts.

Drop ⅓ cup batter at a time onto the hot skillet and cook until the underside is browned, 2-3 minutes. Turn the blinis and cook another minute or 2. Slip browned blinis onto a warm plate and keep in a 200° F. oven while preparing the rest.

Serve blinis on warmed plates with Blackberry Sauce and a dab of sour cream.

YIELD: 12 blinis (4 servings)

French Toast with Plum Sauce

Day-old French bread is never wasted at our house. I turn it into an opportunity to enjoy French Toast, hot, puffed, and browned from the oven. We sprinkle each serving with Vanilla Sugar and pour on a syrup made from a fruit preserve with an assertive flavor and distinct fruit pieces, such as Spicy Cranberry Jam, or Pear and Grape Preserves (see index).

Toast

> 4 large eggs
> 1 tablespoon sugar
> ½ teaspoon salt
> ¼ teaspoon each: ground cinnamon, nutmeg, ginger
> ¼ teaspoon vanilla extract
> 1 cup light cream
> 8-12 slices dry French bread (4-6 ounces)
> 3 tablespoons unsalted butter
> 2 tablespoons vegetable oil
> ¼ cup Vanilla Sugar (recipe follows)

Vanilla Sugar

   1 6-inch-long vanilla bean
   1 cup granulated sugar

Sauce

   1 Master Recipe for Fruit Sauce using Plum Jam with Cardamom,
      Italian Plum Preserves, or Damson Plum Jam (see index)

Preheat the oven to 425° F.

Toast

   Lightly beat eggs together with a fork in a jelly roll pan. Measure and stir in sugar, salt, spices, and vanilla. Slowly pour in the cream, stirring to mix well.

   Add the bread slices to this custard mixture and let them soak for 3 minutes on each side, until slices are saturated but still hold their shape.

   Combine butter and oil in a 12-inch ovenproof skillet or pan. Place it in the hot oven to heat the fats.

   Lay the soaked slices in the hot fats and bake for 7 minutes. Turn the slices over and bake another 7 minutes.

Vanilla Sugar

   Snip the vanilla bean into ¼-inch segments over the sugar. Pulverize these pieces in the sugar in a food processor or blender.

   Stored in an airtight container, vanilla sugar will keep and become more fragrant for several months.

   Serve French Toast hot from the oven, lightly sprinkled with vanilla sugar. Pass syrup at the table.

YIELD: 4–6 servings

Risen Biscuits

The combination of yeast and baking powder gives these biscuits a high rise and a light texture. The biscuit is firm in the hand and crumbles easily in the mouth. A berry preserve adds just the right amount of texture in the mouth and a wild, woodsy scent to this eating experience. My favorites include Four-Berry Jam, Rhubarb Blackberry Jam, and Blueberry Raspberry Preserves (see index).

If you make the variation of this recipe with fresh herbs, serve the biscuits with a wine or herb jelly (see index).

Biscuit Dough

1 package active dry yeast
¼ cup warm water (100° F.)
½ tablespoon sugar
2½ cups all-purpose flour
½ teaspoon salt
½ teaspoon baking powder
⅓ cup shortening
¾ cup buttermilk at room temperature
½ stick unsalted butter (2 ounces), melted

Dissolve the yeast in water with sugar. Combine flour, salt, and baking powder in a 4-quart mixing bowl. Cut the shortening into a fine, mealy texture with the dry ingredients. Pour on the foamy yeast and buttermilk and beat into a stiff dough. Turn out the ball of dough onto a lightly floured work surface and knead by hand 1–2 minutes, until it is taut and springy. Cover and let it rest for 15 minutes. (Cut shortening into dry ingredients with rapid on-and-off motions in a food processor. Add yeast and buttermilk, then process until dough starts to ball. Knead by hand.)

Roll the dough out ½ inch thick and cut into 2-inch rounds with a biscuit cutter. Baste half the biscuit bottoms with melted butter. Place the other biscuit rounds on top. Spread biscuits 2 inches apart on a buttered and floured baking sheet. Cover them with plastic wrap and let rise in a warm, draft-free spot for 1 hour.

Preheat the oven to 375° F. Bake for 12 minutes or until richly browned. Cool the biscuits briefly on a wire rack and serve warm.

YIELD: 14 biscuits

Risen Herb Twist Biscuits

This is a variation of Risen Biscuits

Herb Twist

    ½ cup minced fresh herbs
    ½ teaspoon dried thyme, powdered
    ½ teaspoon powdered ginger
    1 large egg yolk beaten with 1 tablespoon water
    Biscuit Dough (see preceding recipe)

While the dough rests after kneading, collect fresh and dry herbs. Clip the fresh ones into small pieces and toss together. Roll the biscuit dough into an 8-by-12-inch rectangle. Brush the beaten egg yolk over the entire surface and sprinkle on the herbs and ginger. Roll up the dough along its wider side, brushing more yolk mixture on the exposed underside of the dough as it is rolled up. Tightly pinch the edge closed.

Slice the biscuit roll into 14 pieces with a sharp knife. Space the rolls 2 inches apart on a prepared baking sheet, cover with plastic wrap, and let them rise in a warm, draft-free spot for 1 hour.

Brush the biscuits with the remaining egg yolk wash and bake as directed in the Risen Biscuits recipe above.

YIELD: 14 biscuits

Master Recipe for English Muffins

Homemade English Muffins, eaten warm, are simply light years away from the dry sponges that pose as muffins in the supermarket. They are so simple to assemble, it's a wonder homemade muffins aren't the norm. Of all the breads tested for this book, this was my family's favorite.

It's their yeasty aroma and chewy texture that make English Muffins unique. I serve them with all the preserves with texture and tangy flavor.

1 package active dry yeast
1 tablespoon sugar
¾ cup water
1 cup milk
1½ cups unbleached white flour
1½ cups bread flour
2 teaspoons salt
1 cup cornmeal

Dissolve yeast and sugar in ½ cup warm water (100° F.). Let a foam develop. Warm milk to tepid (70° F.).

Mix flours and salt together in a 3-quart bowl. Pour in the yeast mixture, milk, and as much of the remaining ¼ cup water as is needed to make a thick batter. When stirred, the dough will stick in equal parts to the stirring tool and the sides of the bowl. Beat for 3 minutes by hand or in an electric mixer until the dough is quite elastic.

Let the dough rise, covered, in a protected spot at 75° F. until it doubles. This will take about 1 hour.

Heat a steel griddle or a heavy 12-inch skillet. Pour ½ cup cornmeal on a clean work surface. Punch down the risen dough and pull off a ½-cup piece. It will be sticky and stretchable. Coat it lightly with cornmeal for easier handling, shape it into a flattened disk, and set it in a muffin baking ring or free-form on the hot surface. Shape the remaining muffins this way.

Bake muffins 5 minutes on each side. Let them cool for 15 minutes on a wire rack, pull them apart with fingers or fork, and serve warm with sweet butter and preserves.

YIELD: 12 English muffins

English Muffin Variations
Whole Wheat English Muffins

Substitute 1 cup whole wheat flour for 1 cup unbleached white flour in the master recipe above.
Follow the same directions as for the master recipe.

Buckwheat English Muffins

Substitute ½ cup each buckwheat and whole wheat flour for 1 cup white flour in the master recipe above.
Follow the same directions as for the master recipe.

English Muffins with Yogurt

One way to flatter a sweet preserve is to serve it with a slightly tart bread. Instead of making a sourdough bread, which is a considerable undertaking, I added feta cheese and yogurt to the easy English Muffin recipe. When you eat this yogurt muffin along with sweet butter, savor the added dimension its lightly sour element brings to this yeasty, chewy bread. Serve it with Strawberry Preserves or Italian Plum Preserves (see index).

    1 tablespoon active dry yeast
    1 tablespoon sugar
    1 cup warm water
    1½ cups bread flour
    1½ cups unbleached white flour
    2 teaspoons salt
    4 ounces feta cheese, grated
    1 cup plain yogurt
    Cornmeal

(Recipe continues on following page.)

Dissolve yeast and sugar in ½ cup warm water (100° F.). Let a foam develop.

Combine flours and salt in a 3-quart bowl. Make a well in the center of the dry ingredients and add grated cheese, yogurt, yeast mixture, and remaining water. Gradually stir dry ingredients into the wet to make a thick batter. When stirred, the dough will stick in equal parts to the stirring tool and the sides of the bowl. Beat by hand or in an electric mixer for 3 minutes, until the dough is quite elastic.

Let the batter rise, covered, in a protected place at 75° F. until it doubles. This will take about 1 hour.

Heat a steel griddle or a heavy 12-inch skillet. Pour ½ cup cornmeal onto a clean work surface. Punch down the dough and tear off a ½-cup piece. It will be sticky and stretchable. Coat it lightly with cornmeal for easier handling, shape it into a flattened disk, and set it in a metal muffin ring or free-form on the hot surface. Shape the remaining muffins this way.

Bake muffins for 5 minutes on each side. The tops will darken considerably. Let them cool for 15 minutes on a wire rack, split them open with fingers or fork, and eat warm with sweet butter and preserves.

YIELD: 14 muffins

9

DESSERTS

This chapter has been an integral part of my book from its very conception. Why leave your delicious preserves on the breakfast table when they could become important ingredients in wonderful desserts?

My search for compatible ingredients quickly showed the natural affinity fruit preserves have for butter, flour, eggs, and cream—especially when combined in pastry and custard. Rich, bland ingredients showcase the strongly sweet-sour, sometimes slightly bitter character of fruit preserves. Therefore I have included in this chapter recipes for basic custard, pastry dough, spongecake, cultured cream, and simple syrup separately, ready to be used individually as well as in a variety of contexts.

A collection of English cookbooks supplied inspiration for many combinations of these elements. For example, there is a tradition among English housewives of showing off preserves by filling a single pastry shell with samples of many jams, each separated from the others by a lattice crust. I have modified that demanding practice by suggesting seven single jam, preserve, or marmalade fillings for an 11-inch pastry shell. In place of the lattice crust, each filling is paired with a delectable ring of complementary fresh fruit slices as a garnish. Use the fillings presented here and then try your own ideas.

In another quick adaptation from English cooking, I took homey, reassuring bread pudding and slathered jam on one side of the slices before pouring on custard and baking. Yes, it is as easy to make as it sounds.

The fruit fool is an equally trouble-free dessert of cooked and sweet-ened fruit folded into whipped cream. The supertart green gooseberry is the fruit of choice in England, but it's hard to find in America. I have used rhubarb, though many of the berry jams or preserves would be good here as well.

The sturdy English trifle is a rich favorite of mine that combines sherry-soaked cake and preserves with a rich custard filling. There is a beautiful Strawberry Trifle (see index) in this collection. I have filled a rolled sponge-cake with preserves, sliced the roll, and then laid the pieces side by side in a decorative glass bowl to form a design of repeated crimson spirals. The Orange Bread Pudding (see index) will please those who like the stronger flavors of marmalade layered between white and seedless rye bread soaked with sherry and a Grand Marnier-flavored custard.

The closest American translation of the English pudding is cheese-cake. I have chosen to use Spicy Blueberry Preserves (see index) as a topping for a creamy filling. Roasted pecans in the crust add scent and crunch that are flattering to the other ingredients. By simply changing the topping flavor and choice of nuts (replace the pecan sandies with graham crackers or vanilla wafers), you can improvise new, wonderful taste experi-ences.

The classic Austrian Linzer Torte (see index), a jam-filled nut tart, is another obviously good use for homemade preserves. Homemade Red Raspberry Preserves (see index) make it an exciting taste treat. I have altered the traditional recipe by crushing hazelnuts instead of almonds for the crust. You could also use pecans or walnuts with a filling of firm Cherry Preserves with Cassis or Apple Ginger Jam (see index). It would not be a Linzer Torte anymore, but who would care?

My experiments in freezing fruit preserves with eggs and cream as well as with a simple syrup (a light sugar and water solution) resulted in easy formulas for exciting new ice cream and sorbet flavors. Would you ever find a plum jam with cardamom ice cream or a rhubarb ginger sorbet in a supermarket or a cherry and red raspberry ice cream at your local ice cream shop? Actually, there are two basic ice cream recipes here: one custard style and another, called Philadelphia-Style Ice Cream (see index), which com-bines preserves simply with light cream. The sorbets are so thick with fruit they can be soft-frozen on a tray. You may take your choice of any jam or fruit preserve to create a wonderful frozen dessert.

What does a heated preserve taste like? Try my hot dessert soufflé formula and find out how glamorous marmalades and preserves can be. You can serve this beautiful cloud-light soufflé with its purée of red raspberries slowly and calmly at the table because it will not fall; the technique is failsafe.

One last, and perhaps the most obvious, role for jams and jellies is in a complementary sauce for fresh fruit. Sauces are made according to a simple formula with Simple Syrup (see index). Each receives a congenial liqueur matching the fruit it accompanies. In the Fresh Pears with Blackberry Sauce (see index) a little pear brandy is stirred into the sauce. The Baked Peach Halves with Blueberry Sauce (see index) suggests both cassis and lemon juice. My Fresh Peach Melba recipe (see index) combines fresh peach slices with a frozen light cream and warm fragrant raspberry sauce.

Homemade preserves can introduce you to a whole new realm of fruit desserts that will complement your menus during all seasons of the year.

Fresh Pears with Blackberry Sauce

This is a wonderful last-minute dessert for family and guests. If you have time to prepare the pears an hour or two before dinner, the syrup will protect their color and freshness in the refrigerator. The sauce is so easy that it invites improvisation. How about a quick infusion of fresh mint or lemon verbena, plus a sprig as garnish on each plate?

6 firm, ripe pears
2 cups Simple Syrup (see index)
⅔ cup Blackberry Ginger Preserves, No-Sugar Apple Blackberry Jam, Blueberry Blackberry Preserves, or Spicy Blueberry Preserves (see index)
2 tablespoons blackberry brandy or 1 teaspoon fresh lemon juice

Peel and halve the pears. Remove stems and blossom ends with a paring knife. Scoop out cores with the small cup of a melon-baller.

Lay halves in a shallow bowl filled with the syrup. Coat them well and chill. (They may be prepared 2-3 hours in advance but not overnight.)

At serving time, lift the pears onto shallow dessert dishes, 2 halves per serving.

Combine preserves with ⅓ cup of the syrup in a small skillet. Warm enough to make a smooth sauce. Add the brandy or lemon juice and simmer 30 seconds.

Spoon the warm fruit sauce over the pears and serve immediately.

YIELD: 6 servings

Baked Peach Halves with Blueberry Sauce

When the Michigan peaches appear at the farmers' market in August, I always search out a few large, impeccably ripe beauties to bake. They seem to sweeten in the oven with their stuffing of nuts, blueberries, macaroon crumbs, and a wonderful black currant liqueur called cassis. Served at room temperature with a warm, delicate blueberry sauce, these peach halves are simple summer eating at its best.

Peaches

    2 tablespoons chopped pecans
    6 ripe freestone peaches
    ⅓ cup crumbled macaroon cookies
    ¼ cup fresh blueberries
    ¼ cup crème de cassis (black currant liqueur)

Sauce

    ½ cup Spicy Blueberry Preserves or Blueberry Jam with Mint (see index)
    2 tablespoons Simple Syrup (see index)
    1 tablespoon fresh lemon juice
    1 tablespoon crème de cassis

Peaches

Preheat the oven to 350° F. Generously butter a large, shallow baking dish.

Toast the pecans on a baking sheet in the oven for 5 minutes.

Halve the peaches, remove the pits, and enlarge the holes in each half with a melon-baller or spoon, saving the scooped-out flesh.

Crush together these small peach pieces with the macaroons, warm nuts, blueberries, and 2 tablespoons of cassis. Fill the craters of each half with this stuffing. Arrange peaches in the buttered pan so they are not touching. Baste each lightly with 1 tablespoon cassis and bake for 30 minutes. Remove them from the oven and let them cool in the pan.

Sauce

Warm the jam or preserves with the syrup in a small saucepan. Add the lemon juice and cassis.

Serve the peaches at room temperature with the warm sauce.

YIELD: 6 servings

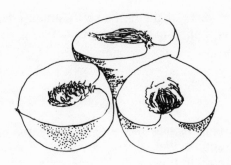

Fresh Peach Melba

This is the perfect dessert to eat when the weather is hot and you have an excess of superripe peaches. The combination of flavors and temperatures is incomparable: cold rich ice cream; sweet, fresh peaches; and warm, tart raspberries. It's a dessert I long for during the winter months.

Ice Cream

⅓ cup superfine sugar
¼ teaspoon vanilla extract
2 cups half-and-half (light cream)

Raspberry Sauce

1 Master Recipe for Fruit Sauce Using Raspberry Jam (see index)
1-2 tablespoons raspberry brandy (optional)

Fruit

6 perfect ripe peaches

Ice Cream

Stir the sugar and vanilla into the cold cream. Freeze this base according to the instructions that accompany your ice cream freezer. Allow 2 hours for the ice cream to mellow in the freezer before serving.

Raspberry Sauce

Make a recipe of the Fruit Sauce, adding the brandy, if desired, and let cool.

Assembly

Dip the peaches in boiling water for 30 seconds. Cool under running water, peel, halve to remove the stones, and thinly slice.

Divide peach slices among 6 glass serving bowls or goblets. Place a generous scoop of ice cream on the fruit. Top each serving with 3 tablespoons warm Raspberry Sauce. Serve immediately.

YIELD: 6 servings

Lemon Amaretto Soufflé with Raspberry Sauce

Here is a soufflé you can serve with panache, right at the table, without having to rush. The soufflé does not collapse immediately because the egg whites have been stabilized with sugar.

Serving the light soufflé hot and the sweet-tart sauce cool heightens the interplay of flavors.

Soufflé

½ cup Lemon Ginger Marmalade (see index)
3 tablespoons Amaretto
5 large egg whites (⅔ cup) at room temperature
¼ cup sugar

Raspberry Sauce

1 10-ounce package frozen red raspberries in sugar syrup
1½ tablespoons crème de cassis liqueur *or* superfine sugar
1 teaspoon strained fresh lemon juice
12 perfect red raspberries

Soufflé

Generously butter and sugar a 6-cup soufflé mold. Refrigerate it.
Preheat the oven to 375° F.
Mix the Lemon Ginger Marmalade with Amaretto in a 2-quart bowl.

Beat whites to soft peaks. Whisk in sugar 1 tablespoon at a time to make a firm meringue. Stir one-third of the whites into the marmalade mixture. Fold in remaining whites in two parts. To fold, make a circular motion with a rubber spatula straight down into the center of the whites, flat along the bottom, and up the side, lifting whites to cover the added ingredient on the surface before returning to the center again. Turn this circle into a doughnut shape by turning the bowl and repeating this action until only streaks of the ingredient being added still show.

(Recipe continues on following page.)

Gently spoon the mixture into the chilled mold and bake for 15 minutes. (Soufflé may be held in the refrigerator for 30 minutes before baking.)

Sauce

Defrost the raspberries and sieve the berries with their syrup to remove the seeds. Stir in the cassis or superfine sugar and lemon juice. Refrigerate until serving time.

Serving

Serve soufflé hot at the table. (This soufflé will not fall quickly, so it is perfect for presenting and serving at the table.) Surround each serving with cool raspberry sauce and a few fresh berries.

YIELD: 4 servings

Orange Soufflé

½ cup Orange Marmalade II or III (see index)
3 tablespoons Grand Marnier

Substitute Orange Marmalade for Lemon Ginger Marmalade and the Grand Marnier for Amaretto. Proceed with directions for the preceding recipe.

YIELD: 4 servings

Bread and Jam Pudding

This version of the classic bread pudding combines a light cream custard, sturdy bread, sweet butter, and a homemade jam, all of which recall the innocent pleasures of a child's palate. Or perhaps one never outgrows the need to be comforted by such simple, honest ingredients.

Bread

18-24 slices day-old French bread (10-12 ounces)
5 tablespoons softened butter
1¼ cups jam such as Rhubarb Blackberry, Cherry and Red
    Raspberry, Double Black Raspberry, or Strawberry Rhubarb
    Jam (see index)

Custard

2 large eggs
2 large egg yolks
¼ teaspoon salt
½ teaspoon vanilla extract
1 tablespoon sugar
1½ cups half-and-half (light cream)
1½ cups milk

Garnish

Crème Fraîche (see index)
Fresh berry or fruit slices to match the preserves used (optional)

Generously butter an 8-by-12-inch gratin dish.

Preheat the oven to 325°F.

Slice the bread ½ inch thick and butter all slices on one side. Place half the slices at the bottom of the baking dish, butter side down. Cut some slices to fill in spaces between slices as needed.

Cover the slices generously with the jam or marmalade. Then lay on the other half of the slices, butter side up.

Assemble the custard in a 2-quart bowl, adding the ingredients in the order they are listed. Stir the eggs together, stir after seasonings have been added, and stir again as cream and milk are poured. Ladle the custard over the layered bread.

Allow the bread to sit for 20 minutes to absorb the custard. Press the top layer lightly with fingertips to gauge how well the custard has penetrated and to encourage absorption.

Bake for 30 minutes in the upper half of the oven.

Let the pudding cool to warm before serving. Serve with Crème Fraîche and fresh fruit or berry pieces, if desired.

YIELD: 8–10 servings

Orange Bread Pudding

The idea of a dessert combining sweet, sour, and bitter flavors in a creamy pudding was inspired by a most satisfying cabinet pudding I was served at Jovan restaurant in Chicago 10 years ago. A dark strata of rye bread woven into the white added sour overtones to the creamy, custard-saturated loaf. The pudding floated in a lightly bitter caramel and sherry sauce studded with raisins.

1 Recipe English Custard (see index) made with ¼ cup Grand Marnier
12 ounces sandwich bread, crusts trimmed
8 ounces seedless rye bread, crusts trimmed, cut into ½-inch cubes
1 cup Orange Marmalade I *or* other Orange Marmalade recipe (see index)
½ cup sherry
1 cup whipped cream or Crème Fraîche (see index)

Make the custard, adding the Grand Marnier in place of vanilla extract.

Use breads that are a day old and beginning to dry. Generously spread the sandwich loaf slices with marmalade.

Line the bottom and a third of the way up the sides of a 2½-quart decorative glass dish with the sandwich slices, marmalade sides facing up. Add half the rye cubes and sprinkle with ¼ cup sherry. Pour on ¾ cup English Custard.

Make a layer of sandwich bread slices over this. Put on the remaining rye cubes, ¼ cup sherry, and 1 cup custard.

Lay on a final layer of white bread slices, marmalade sides down, and pour on the remaining custard.

Cover the trifle with a round of waxed paper. Find a plate that fits snugly on top of the pudding and set a 4-pound weight on it. Refrigerate the weighted dish for several hours or overnight.

At serving time, remove the weight, plate, and wax paper. Cover the top of the trifle with a layer of whipped cream or Crème Fraîche.

YIELD: 10 servings

Jam Tarts

A tart filled with one of your own preserves and garnished with fresh fruit offers a unique taste combination of buttery crust, moist, sweet and sour fruit filling, and the natural crunch of fresh fruit. If the fruit is lightly washed with melted homemade jelly and the surface glazed briefly under a broiler, the effect is picture perfect.

> 1 prebaked 11-inch Tart Pastry shell (see index)
> 1½ cups (12 ounces) jam, preserves, or marmalade (see list below)
> 1-2 whole fruits, thinly sliced, *or* 1 pint berries (see list below)
> ⅓ cup Red Currant, Cinnamon Cranberry-Apple, or Wine Jelly (see index), melted

Preheat the broiler.

Spread the preserves in an even layer on the tart shell.

Prepare a fruit complementary to the filling: Peel, core, and thinly slice apples. Peel and cut segments from oranges or grapefruits. Cut other fruits or berries into bite-sized pieces. Spread slices in a layered wreath over the preserves. Dot whole berries over the top.

Brush the fruits lightly with melted jelly. Turn the removable outer rim of the springform pan on top of the tart so a ring of metal covers the edges of the crust or they will burn in the broiler. Slide the tart under the broiler until it browns lightly.

Remove the springform protector and cool the tart to room temperature before serving.

Suggested Flavor Combinations

1. Apple Red Raspberry Preserves with apple slices and Cinnamon Cranberry Apple Jelly glaze

2. Apple Grape Preserves with apple slices and Cinnamon Cranberry Apple Jelly

3. Any of the berry preserves or jams with fresh berries and Red Currant Jelly

(Recipe continues on following page.)

4. Kiwifruit Mint Jam with kiwifruit and strawberry slices and Apple or Cinnamon Cranberry Apple Jelly

5. Raspberry Pear Jam with pear slices and Apple or Cinnamon Cranberry Apple Jelly

6. Orange Marmalade with orange segments and strained marmalade instead of jelly

7. Orange Cranberry Marmalade with orange segments and Cinnamon Cranberry Apple Jelly

8. Grapefruit Marmalade with grapefruit segments and strained marmalade instead of jelly

YIELD: 8–12 servings

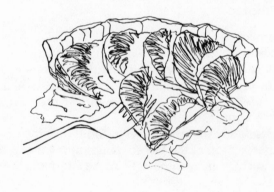

Rhubarb Ginger Fool

A fruit fool is an English dessert as rich as any pudding and originally considered to be a light bit of foolishness at the end of the meal. Its high-quality ingredients and easy assembly make it perfect as a quick party dessert.

The rich cream in a fool requires an acidic fruit preserve partner. My favorite choices are Cherry and Red Raspberry Preserves and Red Raspberry Jam (see index). Any of the jams with rhubarb or blackberry would also taste wonderful.

1 cup Rhubarb Ginger Jam (see index)
⅓ cup Simple Syrup (see index)
Fresh lemon juice
1½ cups pasteurized whipping cream (see note)
2 tablespoons crystallized ginger, cut into thin strips

Stir the jam and syrup together and season with lemon juice to balance sweet with sour tastes.

Beat the cream to soft peaks and spoon it into a 1-quart decorative glass bowl. Fold the jam mixture into the cream incompletely so streaks of pink alternate with white. To fold, make a circular motion with a rubber spatula straight down into the center of the whites, flat along the bottom, and up the sides, lifting whites to cover the jam. Turn this circle into a doughnut shape by turning the bowl and repeating this action until the ingredients are mixed.

This can be made several hours ahead and held in a serving bowl or in individual goblets.

Scatter on ginger strips at serving time.

Note: You must use the richest cream available in your area, at least 32 percent butterfat and hopefully closer to 40 percent. The recipe specifies pasteurized cream because ultrapasteurized cream will not whip properly (or take a culture, for that matter). If you wish to substitute Crème Fraîche, go ahead; it will taste all the better for it. (Be careful when beating a cream mixture that contains Crème Fraîche, for it thickens very rapidly.)

YIELD: 6 servings

Blueberry Pecan Cheesecake

All your preserves and textured jams make delicious garnishes for cheesecake; use this recipe as a formula for any number of innovative combinations (see variations below).

Crust

½ cup pecan halves
10 ounces pecan sandies cookies
4 tablespoons unsalted butter, melted

Filling

1 cup sugar
1 teaspoon salt
3 tablespoons flour
2 pounds cream cheese
1½ teaspoons vanilla extract (½ tablespoon)
3 large eggs
2 cups sour cream

Topping

1½ cups Spicy Blueberry Preserves, Blueberry Jam with Mint, or Blueberry Blackberry Preserves (12 ounces) (see index)

Preheat the oven to 350° F.

Crust

Crush the pecans and cookies together. Sprinkle on the melted butter and toss with crumbs to distribute the fat. (Reduce to fine crumbs in a food processor or blender with rapid on-and-off motions. Sprinkle on the butter and process for 5 seconds.) Press crust mixture into the bottom and up two-thirds of the sides of a 9-inch springform pan.

Refrigerate the pan while assembling the filling.

Filling

Measure sugar, salt, and flour into a 1-quart bowl. Stir them together until they are well blended. Stir them into the cream cheese in a 3-quart bowl. Add the vanilla and the eggs, 1 at a time, stirring to keep mixture smoothly blended. Work in the sour cream 1 cup at a time. (Blend sugar, salt, and flour in a small bowl. Add them to cream cheese and blend in an electric mixer for 1 minute or in a food processor for 15 seconds. Scrape down the sides of the workbowl. Add remaining ingredients with either machine running. Once they are all added, stop the machine again to scrape down the sides. Mix 20 seconds more in the mixer, 10 seconds in the processor.)

Pour the filling into the chilled crust and bake for 50 minutes. The cake's top should be puffed, firm, and lightly browned.

Cool the cake on a wire rack for 30 minutes. Run a knife along the inside of the collar before releasing and removing it. When cake has come to room temperature, chill it until serving time.

Topping

Spoon preserves into the slightly depressed center of the cake. Chill for 30 minutes before serving.

YIELD: 16–20 servings

Cheesecake Variations

Use the same cake filling as in the preceding recipe but substitute a different cookie for the crust (omit the pecan halves). Select a preserve garnish that flatters this new cake and crust combination. Try the combinations below or invent your own.

1. Any one of the ginger-spiced jams, such as Rhubarb Ginger Jam or Blackberry Ginger Preserve (see index), would be terrific with a gingersnap cookie crust.

2. Tropical Pineapple Preserves (see index), with its pure vanilla accent, would taste great in tandem with a rich vanilla wafer crust.

Linzer Torte

After you have made this famous torte with your own Red Raspberry Preserves (see index) you will not want to eat it any other way. The refreshing berry tartness of homemade preserves dispels the tooth-chilling sweetness that plagues commercial versions.

I have also made the crust more interesting by substituting hazelnuts for almonds and roasting them to develop their scent. This results in a more fragrant role for the nuts and a memorable taste combination.

Pastry

1 cup raw hazelnuts (5 ounces)
1 ½ cups unbleached flour
⅛ teaspoon cloves
¼ teaspoon cinnamon
⅓ cup sugar
Grated zest of 1 lemon
1 cup unsalted butter (2 sticks)
2 ounces cream cheese
2 large egg yolks
½ tablespoon vanilla extract

Filling

1 ½ cups Red Raspberry Preserves, Four-Berry Preserves, *or* Cherry and Red Raspberry Jam (see index)

Glaze

1 egg
2 teaspoons cream

Garnish

¼ cup confectioners sugar

Butter a 9-inch springform pan. Preheat the oven to 350° F.
Toast the hazelnuts in the oven for 10 minutes. Rub the warm nuts in a tea towel to remove their brown skins.

Combine the nuts with flour, spices, sugar, and lemon zest (removed with a grater) in the workbowl of a blender or food processor. Pulverize the nuts with the other dry ingredients. (You can also crush the nuts with a mortar and pestle before mixing with the dry ingredients.)

Quarter the sticks of butter lengthwise and cut each stick into 8 pieces across. Cut the cream cheese into teaspoon-sized bits. Blend these cold fats, along with the egg yolks and vanilla, into the dry ingredients with rapid on-and-off motions in a processor or blender. (If you are mixing by hand, warm the butter and cream cheese to room temperature. Cream the fats with eggs and vanilla, then work in the dry ingredient mixture.)

Shape the dough into a flat disk, lightly flour it, wrap it airtight, and chill for 1 hour.

Remove the dough from the refrigerator. Cut off one-quarter of the dough, wrap it, and return it to the refrigerator. Press the larger piece of dough evenly into the bottom and all the way up the sides of the pan.

Spread the preserves on the dough.

Take out the remaining piece of dough and roll it about ¼-inch thick on a lightly floured surface. Cut ½-inch strips and lay some parallel at 1½-inch intervals on the preserves. Turn the pan 90 degrees and repeat the parallel strips to form a lattice. Use a paring knife to bend the dough above the raspberry layer away from the sides of the pan. Press them onto the raspberry layer to make a thick border around the pan, sealing and framing the lattice.

Beat together the egg and cream. Baste all pastry surfaces with this glaze and refrigerate the torte for ½ hour.

Bake for 45 minutes or until the tart is richly browned. Let the cake cool 10 minutes before removing the springform sides.

Dust the top with confectioners sugar. Slide the torte off the pan bottom onto a serving tray when it has come to room temperature.

YIELD: 10–12 servings

Strawberry Trifle

After sampling this strawberry cake roll saturated with rich custard and decorated with whipped cream you will be surprised to learn that the word trifle *originally meant an offering of little consequence.*

1 sheet Jelly Roll Spongecake (see index)
½ cup medium-sweet sherry
1½ cups Strawberry Preserves (see index)
1½ recipes of English Custard (see index)
1 cup whipped cream

Remove the waxed paper protecting the top surface of the cake. Trim edges and sprinkle the cake with 2 tablespoons sherry.

Spread on the Strawberry Preserves and roll up the cake along the long edge, using the wax paper lining the bottom to guide it. Cut the jelly roll cake into 14 1-inch-thick slices.

Line a 2-quart glass serving bowl with the jelly roll slices. Sprinkle the remaining sherry over the slices.

Pour on the English Custard. Layer the top of the custard with the remaining jelly roll slices.

Cover and chill at least 2 hours before serving. (It can be held for several hours or overnight.)

At serving time, pipe whipped cream with a rosette tip in a decorative pattern over the top. (You can also spoon out the trifle and add a dollop of whipped cream to each plate as it is served.)

YIELD: 10 servings

Master Recipe for Fruit Sorbets

I was delighted to find that homemade preserves taste wonderfully fresh as frozen ices. It must be the result of their concentrated flavor and moderate sugar content. Another pleasant surprise was the supple body of these frozen preserves. A diluted jam can be poured onto a baking sheet, left in the freezer compartment of your refrigerator, and scooped out soft-frozen into serving goblets just two hours later. No ice cream machine is necessary. These sorbets also retain their shape well and do not separate in storage.

> **2 cups fruit jam, no-sugar jam, or berry preserve**
> **2 cups Simple Syrup (see index)**
> **1 tablespoon (or more) fresh lemon or lime juice**

Combine a jam or preserve with an equal volume of syrup. Stir them together. Add lemon or lime juice to balance the sweetness with a bit of tartness.

Freezing in an Ice Cream Machine

Chill the sorbet base. Stir it well and pour into an ice cream machine. Freeze it following the instructions that come with the machine.

Freezing without an Ice Cream Machine

Freeze sorbet on a shallow baking sheet at 0° F. It will be soft-frozen within 2 hours. Spoon into goblets or sherbet glasses and serve immediately.

YIELD: 1 quart

Master Recipe for Philadelphia-Style Ice Cream Made with Preserves

If you like your ice cream light and fruity, this is the formula for you. It provides a good opportunity to use a loose-textured preserve with an assertive fruit flavor such as Nectarine Slices with Grand Marnier, Double Black Raspberry Jam, or Strawberry Blackberry Preserves (see index).

2 cups half-and-half (light cream)
2 cups fruit jam or preserves

Stir cream into jam or preserves.

Chill this mixture for 2 hours. Stir and freeze according to the instructions that accompany your ice cream freezer.

Serve ice cream soft-frozen, fresh from the ice cream machine, or mellow and firm from 2-4 hours in the freezer.

YIELD: 1 quart

Master Recipe for Fruit-Flavored Ice Cream Custard

Pair this recipe's silken, yolk-enriched custard base with one of the more penetrating and luxurious fruit flavors, such as Four-Berry Preserves, Peach Preserves with Raspberries, or Blueberry Jam with Mint (see index).

1 cup half-and-half (light cream)
1-2 cups whipping cream
6 large egg yolks
2 cups jam or preserves

Combine 1 cup half-and-half with 1 cup whipping cream in a heavy, nonreactive 1-quart pan and heat to scalding (180°F.).

Beat the yolks lightly in a 1-quart bowl. Gradually pour in 1 cup hot cream, stirring constantly. Return the yolk-enriched cream to the pan and cook briefly over low heat until the custard coats the spoon (170°F.).

Sieve the custard into a 1½-quart bowl. Stir preserves into the hot liquid and mix until it reaches a smooth consistency. Thin this ice cream base with additional whipping cream to taste. The flavor of the fruit should remain strong.

Refrigerate this base until it is thoroughly chilled, 2-4 hours. Freeze according to the instructions that accompany your machine.

YIELD: 1½ quarts

Simple Syrup

Simple Syrup is used to dilute a fruit preserve so it can be poured as a sauce or soft-frozen. The tablespoon of lemon juice in the syrup acts as a catalyst to dissolve the sugar.

3 cups water
1 cup granulated sugar
1 tablespoon strained fresh lemon juice

Combine water, sugar, and lemon juice in a heavy, nonreactive 2-quart saucepan. Heat, stirring occasionally, until the sugar dissolves.

Let the syrup cool to room temperature and transfer it to a storage jar. It will keep, refrigerated, as long as 2 months. Use as needed to thin preserves and jams for sauces and frozen desserts.

YIELD: 4 cups

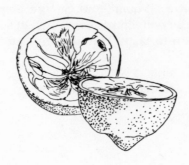

Master Recipe for Fruit Sauce Made with Jams and Preserves

Although proportions are specified in this recipe, you may use them with flexibility, thinning fruit preserves to the consistency you desire for each dessert. Add lemon juice 1 teaspoon at a time, tasting after each addition, until you reach a balance of sweet and sour elements.

1½ cups fruit jam or preserves
½ cup (or more) Simple Syrup (see index)
Fresh lemon juice to taste

Heat jam or preserves with ½ cup Simple Syrup in a heavy, nonreactive 1-quart saucepan, stirring constantly until the mixture forms a smooth sauce. Thin with additional syrup if the sauce is too thick to coat a spoon lightly and evenly.

Off the heat, add lemon juice by the teaspoon to balance the sweetness of the sauce.

Serve warm or at room temperature with ice cream, fruits, cakes, French toast, or blinis.

YIELD: 2 cups

Tart Pastry

You will find this pastry dough reliably firm and supple for rolling and spreading in a pan. It bakes to a crisp crust that crumbles easily in the mouth, emitting a warm buttery flavor.

1 ½ cups unbleached flour
¼ teaspoon salt
1 stick (4 ounces) cold unsalted butter
2 ounces cold cream cheese
1 egg, beaten
2 tablespoons melted jelly (use the flavor that will glaze the fruit)

Assembling the Dough

Measure and mix flour and salt in a 2-quart bowl. Quarter the cold butter lengthwise and cut across into 8 pieces. Separate the cream cheese into ½-tablespoon pieces. Scatter the fats over the flour and work them in with a pastry blender or fingertips until the mixture is mealy. (Use rapid on-and-off motions to cut fat into flour using a steel blade in the food processor. Stir the fats in with the paddle attachment in an electric mixer.)

Add the beaten egg and mix into the other ingredients until a ball begins to form. Turn out the dough pieces onto a lightly floured work surface and alternately press and smear them together with the palm of your hand until the dough is smooth and blended.

Shape the dough into a flat rectangle and lightly flour it. Wrap it in wax paper and chill for 1 hour.

Forming a Crust

Roll out the chilled dough on a lightly floured work surface until it is a 13-inch round. Roll the circle onto the pin and unroll it over an 11-inch springform pan. Fit the dough into the pan by lifting the outer rim of dough toward the center and pressing it lightly along the bottom and up the sides. There will be an extra inch of pastry all around. Turn this excess back over the side so it is a double thickness. Prick the entire bottom of the pastry with a fork at ½-inch intervals. Cover and chill the dough for 30 minutes.

Prebaking the Crust

Preheat the oven to 400° F.

Line the chilled tart shell bottom and sides with wax paper and pour on a generous layer of dry beans or rice to weight it.

Bake the shell on a cookie sheet for 15 minutes. Remove the pastry from the oven and lift out the paper and weight.

Bake shell another 10 minutes. Check every 2-3 minutes and release the air under the pastry with a couple of quick pricks of a fork if it inflates. Bake until the pastry is lightly browned along the upper edge.

Brush a thin layer of melted jelly on the shell bottom and return the shell to the hot oven for another 2-3 minutes, until it dries.

Let the pastry shell cool to room temperature before removing the outer springform ring and proceeding to fill.

YIELD: 1 11-inch springform tart pan or 12–15 shallow 2-inch shells

Jelly Roll Spongecake

A light, lemon-scented spongecake is the perfect partner for a filling of rich strawberry preserves. To make a modern presentation of this jelly roll, serve 3 thin overlapping slices on a dessert plate, surround it with custard, and garnish with fresh berries.

5 large egg whites at room temperature (¾ cup)
Pinch of salt
1 cup granulated sugar
4 large egg yolks at room temperature
¾ cup flour sifted before measuring
1 teaspoon grated lemon rind

Butter the bottom of a 10-by-15-inch sheet cake pan. Line it with wax paper or parchment and butter the paper.

Preheat the oven to 350° F.

Beat the whites to soft peaks with a pinch of salt. Add sugar ¼ cup at a time, continuing to beat as the whites gain body and flexibility. Lightly beat the yolks with a fork and fold them into the whites. To fold, make a circular motion with a rubber spatula straight down into the center of the whites, flat along the bottom, and up the sides, lifting whites to cover the added ingredient on the surface before returning into the center again. Turn this circle into a doughnut shape by turning the bowl and repeating this action until only light streaks of the ingredient being folded still show. Sift on the flour ¼ cup at a time and gently fold it in, adding the grated lemon peel (removed with a grater) with the last of the flour.

Gently ladle the batter onto the cake sheet and level it. Bake for 15 minutes or until the cake is puffed and golden. A toothpick inserted in the cake will come out clean.

Let the cake cool in its pan on the rack. Loosen the cake around the edges and turn it onto a strip of lightly oiled wax paper 6 inches longer than the length of the pan. (If you are not filling this cake immediately, roll it up and store it in an airtight plastic bag in the refrigerator or freezer.

YIELD: 1 10-by-15-inch spongecake

English Custard

This custard formula is rich in egg yolks for extra body and color. Substitute 2 tablespoons of a fruit brandy or liqueur per cup of custard in place of vanilla, if you want the custard to complement a specific fruit flavor.

2 cups half-and-half (light cream)
1 6-inch vanilla bean *or* 1 teaspoon pure vanilla extract
8 egg yolks
½ cup sugar
¼ teaspoon salt

Pour the cream into a heavy, nonreactive 1½-quart saucepan. Cut through the outer peel of the vanilla bean along its length with a paring knife. (Add the vanilla extract while the finished custard is cooling.) Put the bean in the pot and heat the cream to 180° F. This is the point when small bubbles appear at the edge of the pot and a skin forms over the cream.

While the cream is heating, whisk together egg yolks, sugar, and salt in a 2-quart bowl. Slowly pour 1 cup of the hot cream into the yolks, whisking vigorously. Return this mixture and the remaining cream to the pan and heat, stirring constantly, until the custard coats the spoon, about 170° F.

Sieve the custard into a 1-quart measure and remove the vanilla bean. Dot the surface with the end of a stick of unsalted butter to prevent a skin from forming.

After 15 minutes, stir in vanilla extract if you haven't used a vanilla bean. Dot the surface again, cool to room temperature, and refrigerate.

YIELD: 2½ cups

Crème Fraîche

This lightly cultured cream has a slightly sour taste and thickened consistency that complements sweet desserts made with fruit preserves.

2 cups pasteurized whipping cream
2 tablespoons buttermilk

Heat the cream to 100° F. in a saucepan. Pour it into a glass container with a lid that seals tightly. Stir in the buttermilk.

Keep the closed jar at room temperature, between 70 and 75° F., for 18-36 hours, until the cream has thickened noticeably.

Refrigerate this cultured cream and it will continue to thicken, but more slowly at a colder temperature. Plan to use it within a month and stir it well each time before pouring.

YIELD: 2 cups

APPENDIX
A SEASONAL GUIDE TO FRESH FRUITS AND VEGETABLES FOR PRESERVING

Each fruit is listed with the months it is in season. My resource for this task was the *Supply Guide* from the United Fresh Fruit and Vegetable Association, which indicates the availability of produce at wholesale markets rather than their harvest times. Italicized months indicate seasonal peaks.

Many of the ripeness profiles that follow the dating were supplemented by information from *The Greengrocer* by Joe Carcione. I describe the appearance of some fruits when they are underripe to encourage their use in small amounts (25%) to benefit acid and pectin content in jelly, marmalade, and preserves.

FRUITS

APPLE

Cortland: September and October
Golden Delicious: year-round
Granny Smith: all months except October
Greening: October and November
Jonathan: October to May
MacIntosh: October to June
All apples should be firm, well formed, glossy, and free of bruises and blemishes.

APRICOT: late May, *June, July,* and August
Firm, golden, fuzzy fruits are best. A touch of pink blush indicates they are approaching full ripeness.

BLACKBERRY: June, *July, August,* and September
Look for plump, dark blackberries with long caps packed with juicy lobes.

BLUEBERRY: June, *July, and August*
Berries that are full, round, and firm with a dusty bloom are best. Include a few with a reddish tinge, which indicates they are slightly underripe and good for preserving.

B OYSENBERRY: June, *July, and August*
These look like giant blackberries. Both whole berries and clustered lobes are larger and fuller. They are also quite fragile. Avoid baskets stained with juice. Store berries in a single layer and use them within two days.

CHERRY, SOUR: June and July
Cherries should be bright red, slightly soft to the touch, and unblemished, with green stems attached.

CRABAPPLE: July and August
These miniature round apples can vary in color from bright orange gold to dark red. Select large unflawed ones from the tree rather than the ground if you are harvesting them yourself.

CRANBERRY: *October, November,* and December
Color is not as good an indicator of quality as the condition of the fruit. Berries should be oval, firm, and bright, free of dents and soft spots.

CURRANT , RED: July
These small berries should be a rich translucent red, perfectly round and on the stem.

FIG, DRIED: year-round
Choose packages of golden Calimyrna or Calamata figs that are gently firm but not hard or dry to the touch.

GRAPE, CONCORD: September and *October*
Good bunches will have well-developed side branches packed with dark, plump grapes that carry a natural dusty bloom.

GRAPEFRUIT, PINK AND WHITE: October through March
This fruit should be round, firm, and heavy for its size. Peel is best when bright yellow and fine-grained.

KIWIFRUIT: California: October through May
This brown fuzzy fruit is ready for the preserving pot when it is still quite firm, yielding only slightly to gentle finger pressure.

LEMON: year-round
Look for lemons that have a fine-grained skin and bright yellow color with a slightly greenish cast, which is a sign that they are barely ripe and wonderfully sour. Pick ones that are oval, firm, and feel heavy for their size.

LIME: year-round
They will have the same features as lemons: good shape (in this case, round), bright color, no blemishes, and fine grain. A slightly yellowish tinge to the skin indicates ripeness, so choose the less ripe green ones.

NECTARINE: June through September
Nectarines should be bright yellow-gold with a fine red blush, which indicates they are just ripe. They will also be slightly soft along the seam of the fruit. Pick ones that are plump, well formed, and unbruised.

ORANGE, NAVEL: most available November through May
Color is not as good a guide to fruit maturity as the feel of the orange in your hand. You want it to be firm, round, and heavy for its size. The skin should be fine-grained and free from mold and blemishes.

PEACH: May, June, *July, August,* and September
Make sure the peaches you buy have a uniform yellow cast, which indicates they were not picked green. They should be firm but yield a bit to gentle pressure and give off a rich peach fragrance.

PEAR, BARTLETT: August through October
Pears are picked green, and you can purchase them at an early stage of ripening to let them slowly turn golden in your kitchen at room temperature. Use them when they have just turned yellow and before their tender skins give slightly to gentle pressure.

PLUM, ITALIAN: July, August, and September
Ripe Italian plums have a slightly hazy bloom over their dusty purple skins, and their plump oval lobes give under the thin skin. Some can be used for preserving when they are still rather firm and reddish in hue.

PLUM, DAMSON: August
Damsons are small, plump, and tender spheres of deep purple.

PINEAPPLE: year-round
The best signs of ripeness in a pineapple are a bright green crown and golden fruit color accompanied by a fragrant fruit scent. However, this ideally

ripe pineapple is a rare find at the supermarket. You'll most likely have to sniff the scent at stem end because the fruit will still be cold from refrigeration. If you find one that is fresh looking and smelling with only the lower third golden and the rest green, take it. The pineapple will continue to ripen satisfactorily in your kitchen. Do not purchase any fruit with brown leaves, soft spots, or a spoiled smell. Also note that a large pineapple has a higher percentage of flesh than a small one.

QUINCE: September, October, and November

The quince is a hard, knobby fruit when ripe. Only a gold cast over a green peel and a luscious apple aroma give any indication of ripeness. Cook them before they begin to shrivel at the stem end and soften to the touch.

RASPBERRY, RED AND BLACK: July, August, and September (black in July only)

The caps of ripe raspberries easily slip off the stem. The lobes are firm, plump, and a richly colored shade of red or glossy blue-black. Do not buy boxes stained with fruit. Slide them out of their boxes onto a flat tray in one layer and use within a day or two.

RHUBARB: year-round, *April and May*

Although hothouse farming and summer gardens have made rhubarb available almost all year long, it still tastes best in the spring, when the first field crops are harvested. Deep red field rhubarb has a slightly tarter flavor than the lighter pink hothouse variety. Either is good for preserving as long as stalks are firm, moist, and free of cuts and bruises.

SERVICEBERRY: June, July, and August

This is a crop you will have to pick yourself. The berries mature over the summer, becoming dark red and drier over time. They are best for preserving in late June and July. You may pluck them from the stem since they are small and not particularly juicy. Look for bright red color and round, plump shape.

STRAWBERRY: April, *May, and June*

Strawberries do not have to be deeply red all over to be good for preserving. In fact, as much as 30 percent can be partly ripe. Small plump ones with bright green caps are preferred for preserves, though large berries may be halved or quartered, if necessary, for uniformity. You can store them as long as three days in a single layer in the refrigerator. Do not remove the caps, or rinse them until you are ready to cook.

VEGETABLES

ONION: year-round

Look for firm young onions. Those that ripen early in the season are usually sweeter than the latecomers. (You will have to ask your produce manager about the source and season of the onions when you buy them.) Onion skins should be dry, the flesh firm. Stay away from those whose neck ends are soft, discolored, or sprouting green stems.

PEPPERS

GREEN AND RED BELL: year-round

JALAPEÑO: August through May

Bell and variety peppers can now be had many months of the year, though the jalapeños are more likely available at ethnic markets in the winter. Select those most brightly colored with a smooth glossy surface. Turn them over in your hand to check for undesirable impact bruises and splits.

SQUASH

ZUCCHINI: year-round

Like the other vegetables listed here, zucchini is now available most months of the year. Small zucchini are preferred because they are the most tender throughout. Select ones with a deep green skin, symmetrical oblong shape, and firmness at neck and stem end.

TOMATO

ROUND VARIETIES: July, *August, and September*

ITALIAN PLUM: September and sporadically throughout the winter

Tomatoes taste best when used fresh from the garden in late summer, red ripe and luscious. The best time to select green ones is at the end of the season, before they succumb to frost. The only fresh tomato worth cooking any other time of year is the oval Italian plum that appears for short periods throughout the winter months.

INDEX

A page number in italics indicates an illustration on that page.

225